LESBIAN
(OUT) LAW

Other books by the author:

Eye Of A Hurricane
Cecile

LESBIAN (OUT) LAW

SURVIVAL UNDER THE RULE OF LAW

RUTHANN ROBSON

Firebrand
Books

Ithaca, New York

Portions of this work have appeared in different versions in the *Journal of Law and Equality, Sinister Wisdom, Stanford Journal of Gender, Sexual Orientation, and the Law, Temple Law Review, Texas Journal of Women and Law, Wisconsin Journal of Women and the Law,* and the *Women's Rights Reporter.*

Book design by Betsy Bayley
Cover design by Debra Engstrom
Typesetting by Bets Ltd.

Printed in the United States on acid-free paper by McNaughton & Gunn

Library of Congress Cataloging-in-Publication Data

Robson, Ruthann, 1956–
    Lesbian (out)law : survival under the rule of law / by Ruthann Robson.
        p.   cm.
    ISBN 1–56341–013–3 (cloth). — ISBN 1–56341–012–5 (paper)
    1. Lesbians—Legal status, laws, etc.—United States.   I. Title.
II. Title: Lesbian outlaw.
KF4754.5.R63   1992
346.7301'3—dc20
[347.30613]   92–8333
                                                                   CIP

ACKNOWLEDGMENTS

My mother and father gave me the skills for survival and the stubbornness that sustained me through the research and writing of this book. Although neither of them imagined that their daughter would be either a lesbian or a lawyer, I owe both of these accomplishments to them.

Initial institutional support for this project was provided by the Ll.M. graduate law program of Boalt Hall and the feminist Beatrice M. Bain Research Group, both at the University of California at Berkeley. At Boalt Hall, the support of Reva Siegel, Lisa Orsaba, and Margot Young was vital. The early and continuing enthusiasm and suggestions of fellow Bain-affiliated scholar Jane Caputi have been invaluable.

Institutional support has been provided by the City University of New York (CUNY) Law School at Queens College. In addition to institutional sustenance, the CUNY Law School community has offered an exceptional climate of legal inquiry directed at emancipatory and radical social change—and countless controversies about the contours of that change. Colleagues like Joyce McConnell, Sharon Hom, Victor Goode, and Sidney Harring, and students of incredibly diverse backgrounds and perspectives who have enrolled in seminars on Sexuality and the Law, and Feminist Jurisprudence, have challenged and changed my own theorizing. My thinking about lesbianism within a legal context has benefitted from my work at a law school that takes lesbian concerns seriously and admits a critical mass of outrageous lesbian students.

Members of the CUNY Law School community also made significant contributions to this book by taking the time to engage in conversations on specific topics, or to undertake research. I am grateful to Rebecca Baehr, Guljit Bains, Mary Elizabeth Bartholomew, Beryl Blaustone, Peter DeLizzo, Dawn Dugan, Alphonso

Gaskins, Heidi Li, Carol Martin, Lisa Sbrana, and Amy Whitney. Many lesbian legal workers shared their perceptions of lesbianism and legal work. Lesbians, anonymous and otherwise, completed an informal survey I distributed in 1989. Longer reflections were completed by Marlene Drescher, Deanna R. Duby, Laura Haller, Gretchen James, Jan Lecklinker, Anyda Marchant, Angie Martell, Lisa Orsaba, Dianne Post, and Linda Rothfield. Although I had to abandon my idea of a chapter composed of these reflections, all of them influenced my thinking.

Several women read the draft of this manuscript to insure accessibility, accuracy, and intelligibility. I am indebted to Jane Caputi, Joyce McConnell, Sima Rabinowitz, Lisa Sbrana, and Leslie Thrope for their efforts.

Nancy K. Bereano is a faultless editor and publisher. Her faith in my work, extending from fiction to theory, has been essential; her belief in lesbian and feminist possibilities, expressed both personally and through her tireless work, is inspirational. The work of other lesbians involved in sustaining independent lesbian or feminist presses has also been important. I could not imagine undertaking this work absent such an environment.

Finally, S.E. Valentine has had unwavering confidence in this book from its earliest stages to its final ones, as well as rigorous criticisms throughout all the drafts. I cannot adequately acknowledge her contributions.

Contents

Law, Theory, and Lesbianism

INTRODUCTION

As lesbians, we are both outside the law and within it. And yet, we are always under it. Sometimes under it in the sense of being beneath notice, not deserving of legal recognition. And at other times, under it in the sense of being under a system that dominates, being under its power.

This book is about lesbians under the rule of law that is the American legal system. The *rule of law* is a common description connoting a supposed improvement over the *rule of men*. It is historically true, however, that it is men (and a rather limited class of them) who have created this rule of law. Not surprisingly then, the rule of law mirrors the concerns of the ruling men.

Lesbian (Out)law is concerned with how the rule of men and law impacts upon lesbian survival. By survival, I mean two things. First, the very daily survival that depends on the necessities of life like food, shelter, work, safety, and love. The law denies, or makes very difficult, this type of survival when the rule of law sanctions discrimination in employment and housing, removal of our children, separation from our lovers, and toleration of violence against us.

Second, I mean our survival as lesbians. The law denies, or makes more difficult, this less tangible sort of survival when it defines our lesbianism for us, when it promises us protection and acceptance if we can argue ourselves into its categories.

These two sorts of survival can work at cross-purposes. For example, in order to insure our economic and physical survival, we may argue in a court of law that a lover is equivalent to a spouse and should be entitled to health insurance benefits under a company insurance policy. Our argument is essentially that our lover is "just like" a wife/husband: our lover is expressed and limited to the legal terms set under the rule of law—heterosexual marriage. In making this argument, we might lose our own definition of our lover. If we refuse to argue this way, based on the belief that our lover is nothing like a wife or husband, we might preserve our lesbianism but probably lose the benefits.

Strategizing both types of survival forms the theoretical basis of this book. I am interested in what our relationships to the law and legal process might be. Politically, I reject both assimilationism and separatism as absolute principles. Yet I believe that we must develop a specific lesbian legal theory that allows us to assimilate our lesbianism to law. In doing so, we can make the law responsive to our survival needs. And I also believe that we must resist the way the law denies that we are separate from the rule of men. We must avoid a tendency to think in the dominant legal terms so that our lesbianism becomes colonized, watered-down, and domesticated by legal thinking. Chapter 1 more fully explores the theorizing that could lead us to a lesbian legal theory.

Chapters 2 and 3 discuss the criminalizing of lesbian sexuality. Chapter 2 considers the well-known myth that lesbians were never persecuted or prosecuted for their sexuality, concluding that history is not as benign as we have been led to believe. Chapter 3 considers the present legal text of lesbian sex, and looks at statutes and cases that affect specific lesbian sexual practices.

The next section of the book considers the legal doctrine of privacy and its impact on lesbians. Privacy was the major legal theory advanced in the failed attempt to have the United States Supreme Court declare laws regulating sexual practices unconstitutional. Chapter 4 discusses the case and rhetoric, as well as how privacy is related to the feminist debates regarding pornography. It concludes by discussing how legal notions of privacy impact upon our own supposedly nonlegal discussions about lesbian sexual practices. Chapter 5 explores the publicity of our sexuality, including slander and outing.

Lesbian legal theory as a means to confront the legal regulation of lesbianism is the focus of the next section. Chapters on discrimination, the military, immigration, and imprisonment explore the ways in which the legal regime controls lesbians. Following this, the topic of our relationships is also considered. Chapters on lovers and children discuss concrete applications of lesbian legal theory, often raising more questions than answers. Chapter 13 treats the legal ramifications of the violence against us, and chapter 14 considers the violence among us. Each of these substantive chapters on such seemingly diverse topics can be unbraided into three strands: an analysis of the existing law, an analysis of strategies given the existing law, and the potential for the development of a lesbian legal theory. The final two chapters further consider potentials for change by discussing mediation and lesbian legal workers within the law.

Theory permeates *Lesbian (Out)law,* but by theory I mean thinking focused on the two types of survival. The theoretical inquiry can be stated simply: Can we use the law without being used by it? If so, how can we do that? The responses are complicated and contradictory, but I believe it is important to begin this discussion.

The discussion, it should be clearly stated, is a lesbian one, for I insist on a *lesbian* legal theory, meaning a theory that is inclusively and specifically lesbian. However, much of the substantive discussions of the law will be equally applicable to gay men, and some of the cases discussed involve gay men. The rule of law generally employs the legal/medical category of "homosexual" or in more recent rules of law, the category of "sexual orientation." Despite the rule of law's categorization, I have chosen to center lesbians and lesbian concerns. While *Lesbian (Out)law* has some relevance to gay men, bisexual women and men, heterosexual women, and many other disenfranchised groups, its focus is on lesbians, in all our diversity. The diversity of lesbians means that issues of racism, classism, ableism, ageism, anti-Semitism, and elitism are also often implicated. Additionally, because lesbians are women, issues of sexism become pertinent.

Lesbian (Out)law is intended for a general lesbian audience, as we as for anyone interested in lesbians, law, or theory. Law is not a subject reserved for professionals: it impacts and has the potential to impact each of our lesbian lives. While law and theory are often considered abstract and formidable, they need not be. This book is committed to theorizing in ways that are concrete and accessible. Although I expect that some readers may be familiar with the law, I have nevertheless avoided unnecessary legalisms and endless endnotes. For those interested in more detailed and referenced treatments of particular subjects, the endnotes for each chapter list sources. The legal sources appear in standard legal format. In some cases, there is a reference to a scholarly law review article that I have authored or coauthored. Almost all of the legal sources, including law review articles, statutes, and cases, are available in any law school library. Many of the sources, especially statutes and cases, are available in county, prison, and other law libraries.

This politic of accessibility influences not only the content choices but also the publishing ones. While several university presses are publishing books exclusively in hardcover for lesbian audiences who can afford to pay large sums for slim volumes, *Lesbian (Out)law* is meant to be more widely available. For that reason, it is published by an independent lesbian and feminist publisher, reasonably priced given market conditions, and meant to be read outside of law libraries as well as within them.

This book takes its place beside several fine legal guides and handbooks relating to lesbians and gay men. It is the first book, however, to be specifically lesbian. It is also the first one to seriously and consistently confront lesbian interaction with the law. As such, *Lesbian (Out)law* is not intended to be the definitive text. I would like to begin a conversation rather than have the last word.

In this conversation, each speaker must take responsibility for her questions and conclusions, even tentative ones. Although I have communicated with many lesbians about this work, it remains, like all work, ultimately idiosyncratic. The background for such idiosyncracies bears revealing. I am white and in my thirties. I did not grow up to be a lawyer or having anyone expect I might go to college; I grew up wanting to live to be twenty-one and having many people expect I might not make it. I never knew an attorney until I entered a small private law school on a scholarship at the age of twenty and got a job working for a lawyer, who was later disbarred for stealing clients' money. I graduated law school in 1979, worked for two federal judges in Florida, practiced poverty law, and now teach at one of the very few progressive law schools in the country. My life in the law has been limited by culture (American law), by class (a job rather than career), and by politics (poverty rather than corporate). I have been both a representative of the law and an outlaw, sometimes simultaneously.

Each lesbian reading this book is also both an outlaw and within the law. We each make personal choices about our relationship to the law, based on our own idiosyncracies and biases. We each make decisions about whether or not to pursue certain legal reforms or to denounce them. But we need to confront and consider our choices, and their consequences for lesbianism as we live it, and as we want to live it.

1

DEVELOPING LESBIAN LEGAL THEORY

Developing anything that might be called lesbian legal theory is a risky pursuit these days. As lesbians, we are hardly unified in our approaches to either law or theory. Further, the prevailing intellectual climate of what might loosely be called postmodernism problematizes each side of the theory/law/lesbianism triangle.

Theory as an activity is attacked by many lesbians and postmodernists, usually in a theoretical manner. The most important criticism of theory, it seems to me, is that it is useless. And theory can be useless: meditation at its most abstract and inapplicable. Yet theory is also just another name for thinking, for deciding, for arguing and examining one's own beliefs and principles as well as the beliefs and principles we have been taught. Theorizing is something that we all do.

Yet because we all theorize, another criticism of theory is that it cannot be a singular project. Thus, postmodernist-influenced lesbians condemn Adrienne Rich's "a dream of a common language" because what we should be dreaming about, they say, is a multiplicity of languages, with a multiplicity of voices and accents, probably in a multiplicity of dreams. Applied to dreams about lesbian legal theory, this means that it is arrogantly false to propose anything like a singu-

lar lesbian legal theory. Recognizing the truth of accusations of ar-
rogance levelled at many theorists, however, should not prevent us
from thinking seriously and honestly. Just as Adrienne Rich never
claimed that her dream was the only one, or that the dream was not
subject to constant re-dreaming, theorizing is an ongoing project.

The contemporary postmodernist debates in theory have to
some extent influenced legal theory, although they have had less influence on legal practice. Recent legal scholarship has discussed the
effect of postmodernist practices like deconstruction, arguing against
the stability of any category. However, legal theory has a long history
devoted to its own peculiar concerns. Jurisprudence—the philosophy
of law—was a preoccupation of ancient Greek, Roman, Arabic, and
Chinese thinkers, and its modern expressions have resulted in various philosophical positions such as legal realism, legal positivism, and
naturalism. Current popular schools within legal theory are critical legal studies, law and economics, and feminist legal theory. What all
jurisprudential positions, whether ancient or modern, have in common is some conclusion about the role of law in society: either what
that role is or what that role should be. For example, proponents of
critical legal studies theorize that the law serves powerful social interests that need to be challenged, while members of the law and economics school think that law is simply subject to the same market
forces driving all of society. One's theory about the role of law influences the choices one makes in any legal theory or practice.

Like legal theory, lesbian theory is also subject to current theoretical trends in addition to having its own particular problems. The
category *lesbian* has been subject to intense scrutiny. There are those
who believe the term is only properly an adjective: one can engage
in lesbian-type activities, but one cannot be a lesbian. On the other
hand, there are those who believe lesbian is a specific and discrete category of human, existing cross-culturally and transhistorically. This
division is the lesbian version of the nurture/nature debate, the cho-
sen/born debate, the constructivist/essentialist debate. Its consequences for lesbian theory are apparent every time a lesbian(?) nar-
rates her own life story. The debate also influences what we mean
when we say the word *lesbian*. There are those who believe the term
is a falsely unifying one; that the differences between lesbians as far
as race, class, culture, religion, politics, and even sexual practices are
concerned are so vast, it is nonsense to contemplate a group identity.
And, on the other hand, there are those who believe that despite such
differences between lesbians, there is something important about the
lesbian label, something that may even be important enough to make

other differences less important.

Lesbian, law, and theory are each individual concepts with more than their share of unique philosophical issues. Any attempt to relate these three concepts results in a proliferation of the issues. For example, if my theoretical approach stresses multiplicity, then it will be difficult for me to take a lesbian position on an issue. If the issue is a legal one and my jurisprudential position is in the law and economics mode, I will conduct a cost-benefit analysis before I critique a law. And if the legal issue pertains specifically to lesbians, I will be influenced by my beliefs as to the existence of such essentialist creatures as lesbians who can be protected by antidiscrimination laws. All of these factors, and more, underlie any attempt to discuss lesbian legal theory. My own positions are often hybrids.

Three central concerns emerge, however, from taking the various positions and approaches into account. Vital to the development of any lesbian legal theory are questions about its purposes, its applicability, and its attributes.

Purposes

Developing a theory of law that is specifically lesbian requires clarity about what the purpose of such a theory would be. To say that its purpose is our survival is a start. Any theory that ignores our daily survival is useless. The rule of law does not guarantee our survival, and much of our lesbian legal work has been directed toward making the law more responsive to our needs. Theory can help us decide questions about ultimate goals and strategies. Theory is not a dogmatism that dictates the right and wrong way to protect ourselves if, for example, we have been arrested for kissing a lover in public. Will we risk jail to challenge a legal rule that we believe is being applied disproportionately against lesbians? How do we decide? What would such a challenge mean to our own lives? To other lesbians? Is our decision different if the criminal charges are dropped and we have a choice whether or not to bring our own civil action? Theory can provide an analysis of the various options available to us, enabling us to make choices that might improve our survival, both as human beings and as lesbians.

Yet a lesbian legal theory must also challenge and be self-challenging. To have a lesbian legal theory is not necessarily to have a theory that puts law in the center of lesbianism, or even lesbian efforts at lesbian change. While we have begun to speak about the "therapization" and even the "professionalization" of lesbianism, we must also begin to notice the "legalization" of our lesbian lives. Legalization occurs when we substitute legal categories and concepts for our lesbian ones. This substitution is often unnoticed by us, because we are all part of the legal culture. Americans have a particular penchant for law. As Alex deTocqueville observed about Colonial America: "Judicial language becomes the popular language," and the legal spirit infiltrates "all of society, down to its lowest ranks, and the entire people ends up by adopting parts of the habits and tastes of the magistrates."[1] Surprisingly little has changed in two hundred years. Even for lesbians, the language of the law becomes part of the language we use to communicate with one another.

While this infiltration by law is especially pronounced in American society, the tendency toward regulation and legalism is a hallmark of so-called Western civilization. And like Western civilization, this legalism is imperialist.

Imperialism is just one of the metaphors appropriate to explain this process of legalization. Colonization is another. Yet both imperialism and colonization are more than metaphors, and describe concrete historical processes that have resulted in slavery, death, and destruction. I have come to prefer the term *domestication* to connote this overlegalization of lesbian life. Domestication is a more gendered term. It connotes the relegation of women to the domestic sphere, a private place that can facilitate being dominated and inhibit collective action. It also connotes the circumscribing of one's potential to the service of another, as when animals are domesticated for human use. Like legalization, it is an insidious process that promises not only exploitation but benefits.

Domestication also captures the process inherent in colonization and imperialism of the substitution of one way of thinking for another. Domestication occurs when the views of the dominant culture are so internalized that they seem like common sense. Domestication occurs when the barbed wire enclosures are believed to exist for protection rather than restriction.

Yet domestication also contains within it the idea of its opposite. To have been domesticated, one must have once existed wild: there is the possibility of a feral future. To be feral is to have survived domestication and be transformed into an untamed state. Postdomesticated lesbian existence is one purpose of a lesbian legal theory.

Despite the domestication metaphor, I am not conceptualizing lesbians as women who have been trapped in little houses on the prairie by mean men, or as wild animals who have been harnessed to plow the soybean fields. While these are tempting images that foster an idealized version of our innocence and victimization, such images conflict with my experience. To use the postmodern phrase, we are "always already" domesticated. We are born and socialized with reference to the dominant culture. And because the dominant culture is infiltrated by legal concepts, we also use legalism as part of our common sense. We talk about discrimination, freedom of speech, privacy. We make a contract for a sexual encounter, or dinner, or living together. We want our rights, justice, due process. We are guilty or innocent. We perceive ourselves as victimized by the rule of law and as vindicated by it.

I have problems not only with certain legal concepts, but with how we use legal concepts without thinking. Doing so perpetuates the rule of law, the rule of men. While many of these concepts have roots in political philosophy, they derive a large part of their power from the rule of law in America. When we appeal to legal principles, we assume they are natural and neutral. We often do not stop to think about their sources and what they ultimately represent in terms of lesbian survival.

Lesbian survival is the starting point for developing lesbian legal theory. Of course, we will have many disagreements about the shape of our survival. And even if we agree on these, we will disagree on the strategies to produce them. Yet such disagreements will be the process of developing lesbian legal theory, a process that will not culminate in a theory that can be captured in a single slogan, but one that will shift and change as we do.

Applicability

The continuous movement and rearranging of who we are and how we see ourselves that makes lesbian existence exciting also makes constructing lesbian legal theory difficult. How do we think about ourselves in relation to the law? Are we sexual outlaws, and perhaps political outlaws as well, who recognize that the law is founded upon the rule of men, upon enforced heterosexuality, and upon violence? Or are we legitimate citizens who have been wrongly excluded from legal recognitions and protections because our private lives are slightly different from some mythical norm? These dichotomous opposites—we might say separatist or assimilationist approaches—mark most of our daily relations with law. Each of us may identify more strongly with one or the other, although in the course of a given day we may vacillate between these two poles or embrace them simultaneously. Both are important to lesbians, and thus to any lesbian legal theory. They may, in fact, not be opposites at all, but an ultimatum posed by legal thought that has domesticated lesbian thought. The law's pronouncement that a person is either law-abiding or a criminal may be a dichotomy that serves the law's own interests and does not serve lesbian interests.

Any lesbian legal theory must put lesbians, rather than law, first. Putting lesbians at the center requires a critical attitude toward law. One of the questions posed by a lesbian legal theory is whether or not the law is appropriate in a particular situation. As discussed above, legal concepts can often domesticate lesbian ones, so that our solutions to problems between us become ones imposed by the dominant legal culture rather than ones that best benefit lesbian survival. In applying lesbian legal theory to specific instances, I often distinguish between situations in which all the participants are lesbians, and situations in which some of the participants are nonlesbians.

To say that the rule of law may or may not be applicable depending on the participants counters our conception of fairness and justice. Historically, of course, those with power have been able to determine that established legal concepts like "equality" were not applicable to any person who might be considered a slave, a woman, an immigrant, a prostitute, a laborer, a lesbian, or any combination of the above. Thus, it may appear unjust of us to theorize applying the supposedly neutral principles of law in a less than rigorously neutral manner. If we put lesbians rather than law first, however, the neutrality of the rule of law that is the rule of men becomes suspect. The neutrality of law is, first of all, a pretense. Few people believe that legal principles are like mathematical formulas that can be objectively applied to reach the one and only correct result, free of bias and underlying theoretical positions. Further, neutrality as a good may be questioned from a lesbian perspective. If we put lesbians first, a neutral principle even rigorously applied might disfavor lesbians. For example, a neutral standard like "best interest of the child" applied in child custody cases, as discussed in chapter 11, could result in lesbians who seek custody being denied children because it would not be in the best interests of any child to live with a lesbian mother who will experience discrimination, ostracism, and violence. Legal concepts that sound fair but do not necessarily benefit lesbians can be domesticating if we accept them without challenge.

Putting lesbians first implies an agreement on the need to define lesbians, so we can tell who the people are that we should put first. While the law frequently attempts this definition, often against an individual's own self-definition, we should not allow legal constraints to confine lesbianism. Any such definitions should be lesbian-generated, although we might also reject the notion that definition is needed. I think Cheryl Clarke may have said it best: "A lesbian is a woman who says she is."[2] Although this formulation still has some problems, especially as applied to the past as discussed in the next chapter, it nevertheless provides a starting point. Even recognizing that self-definitions can be socially constructed, or that a certain level of empowerment is necessary to claim any self-definition (especially one that is stigmatized), a lesbian legal theory that applies to those who claim the lesbian label is a beginning for theorizing. What lawyers term the "hard cases," those who engage in lesbian sexual activity but would never self-define as lesbians, for example, or those who claim the lesbian label but are male, can push our theorizing further. We should not refrain from beginning, however, simply because we cannot exhaustively define the parameters of our theorizing.

Lesbian legal theory is grounded in lesbian existence. And even if we cannot capture the category *lesbian* with legal precision, lesbian legal theory—as a nascent project—can be distinguished from other types of legal theory. It is especially important to distinguish lesbian legal theory from the related endeavors of feminist legal theory and the possibility of queer legal theory.

Feminist legal theory has emerged as a force within legal theory. Yet feminist legal theory, perhaps predictably, has been relatively intransigent—even in comparison to academic feminism—when it comes to recognizing lesbian existence. Like other academic feminisms, however, feminist legal theory has been subject to its own divisions and schools, dividing along issues relating to whether women are different from and better than men, or whether women are the same as and equal to men. What becomes apparent in all such debates is that men are used as the legal measure for women. Some of this preoccupation with men accounts for the failure of much of feminist legal theory to address issues of race, age, ability, class, and culture. Gender comparisons have an increased vitality if other comparisons are obscured. (For example, an argument relating to gender equality is much easier to make if the comparison is between a thirty-five-year-old white woman professor teaching American history for five years and a thirty-five-year-old white male professor teaching American history for five years, than if the comparison is between a white woman professor teaching American history for five years and an African-American older male custodian cleaning the floors for five years after having been physically rehabilitated.)

The preoccupation of feminist legal theory with men also leads to the widely shared conclusion that issues of sexual orientation are best conceptualized as issues of gender. In other words, in the realm of discrimination, for example, it is believed that once gender discrimination is adequately addressed, sexual orientation discrimination will have also disappeared. This conviction is displayed by many feminist legal scholars at the same time they bemoan the legal conditions producing travesties like "sex-segregated universities," "more career women not marrying," and "sons not having fathers." Feminist legal theorists also conceptualize lesbians with "their men," i.e., gay men. Astonishing in a discipline that dissects gender in every other aspect of life is the absence of a gendered perspective regarding sexual orientation. For feminist legal scholars, *gay men and lesbians* is a single term.[3]

Considerably less influential than feminist legal theory are the first signs that something like a queer legal theory might be emerging. While there has been considerable discussion of sexual orientation's place in the law, this work has been more about legal doctrine and particular cases than about developing an independent theoretical stance.[4] The risk is that queer theoretical work will mirror queer doctrinal work in perpetuating the invisibility of lesbians. Except for lesbian custody cases, and a few recent discussions of lesbians in the military, most doctrinal legal discussions have focused almost exclusively on gay men. For example, as discussed in chapter 4, the legal commentary to the case in which the Supreme Court upheld a law prohibiting certain sexual practices ignores lesbianism to such an extent that it would seem that the whole issue did not pertain to lesbians. If this trend continues, queer legal theory will in fact be gay male legal theory.[5]

A legal theory that is lesbian puts lesbians at its theoretical center: lesbians of all colors, all classes, all cultures, all abilities, all ages, all politics, all sexual practices, and all spiritualities. While a particular lesbian might find lesbian legal theory inadequate in its applicability to her needs—a lesbian who uses a wheelchair might find the accessibility issues being theorized by disability legal activists more appropriate to a particular goal—a lesbian legal theory cannot segregate a lesbian's disability issues. Thus, although a lesbian legal theory cannot be absolute, it can be coalitional. Opportunities for coalition include not only advancing theoretical approaches to issues such as disability, but also developing theories that definitionally should include lesbianism, such as feminist legal theory and queer legal theory. The insistence on an independent lesbian legal theory is just as necessary if lesbianism is not to be eclipsed by feminist and queer theories. Coalition work is certainly often appropriate, but one cannot be a partner when one is a shadow.

By putting all lesbians at its center, a lesbian legal theory seeks to be applicable to all lesbians. Although its insights might be relevant to others, its focus is unrelentingly on lesbians. Many legal theories attempt to explain all of law for all of time. I do not conceptualize a lesbian legal theory as such a totalization of law. Instead, I desire theory that works toward lesbian survival under the rule of law.

Attributes

If a lesbian legal theory is a theory of law that has as its purpose lesbian survival; if it is relentlessly lesbian and puts lesbians rather than law at its center; if it distinguishes between intralesbian situations and nonlesbian situations; if it is not feminist legal theory and not queer legal theory; if it does not seek to explain the entire enterprise of law, then some of the preliminary work toward developing a lesbian legal theory has begun. Still vague is the content of a lesbian legal theory. Don't we need a list of positive attributes? Some rules, neutral or otherwise? A potluck of principles? Or might we discount any regulatory notions as nonlesbian? Would our theory be entirely process? Communal only? Would there be authority, autonomy, actualization?

In attempting to theorize past the purposes of lesbian survival, I entered the realm of science fiction. Perhaps because of disparities in power, lesbian philosophers like Sappho have bequeathed us fragments of desire, while (gay) philosophers like Plato have left tomes discussing versions of the just society in lengthy dialogues with titles like "Laws" and "The Republic." Contemporary lesbian theorists have likewise been less inclined to hypothesize about the role of law than to discuss love. The few theoretical references to an incipient lesbian law occur in abbreviated dictionarylike entries. Both Monique Wittig and Sande Zeig in *Lesbian Peoples: Material for a Dictionary*[6] and Mary Daly and Jane Caputi in *Websters First New Intergalactic Wickedary of the English Language*[7] place lesbians beyond the law. Wittig and Zeig suggest that "the single law of the amazons was 'do not steal, nor beg'," although many others practiced "do not beg, but steal," and lesbians ancient and modern maintain "abysmal contempt for statutory law." Daly and Caputi relegate the term *law* to the patriarchy, and replace *justice* with *nemesis*, a basis for "internal judgment that sets in motion a kind of psychic alignment of [gyn]energy patterns" which allows one to accomplish "flying through the badlands, badtimes." In both of these conceptions, lesbians react against the dominant legalistic culture by rejecting law.

Lesbian forays into science fiction are similar in spirit. In Joanna Russ' community, Whileaway, for example, the early education of the girl-children is exceedingly practical: "how to get along without machines, law, transportation, physical theory, and so on."[8] In other lesbian futuristic communities, law remains unmentioned, although there are incessant meetings in which decisions seem to be made by consensus. At times, the efficacy of such meetings is assisted immeasurably by telepathic abilities. There is often an appeal to such "natural" communication, especially as contrasted to the artificiality of patriarchal legal codes, as in Sandi Hall's novel *The Wingwomen of Hera*,[9] or a stressing of autonomy in a society of lesbians who value "self-reliance, privacy, respect for each other" and "instinctively oppose authority, uniformity, or any kind of fixity" as in Katherine Forrest's *Daughters of a Coral Dawn*.[10]

In spite of the absence of legal controls, most of the utopian lesbian societies are quite orderly. It is lesbian naturalism, evidenced by instincts and telepathy, that account for this order rather than any coupling of "law and order." Authority in the novels is diffuse, it is usually benevolent and often biologically based. In quite a few lesbian science fiction novels, the "leaders" are accorded their status through birth or attaining old age. While such naturalism is distressing as a principle, conventional lesbian science fiction does reveal that when lesbians imagine a future, they do not imagine law as being an integral part of that future. Thus, if science fiction is any indication, lesbians believe that left to ourselves, we would prefer a nonlegalistic society. Even if we do not accept the novels' essentialist biologic underpinnings—as I find difficult—the overwhelming rejection of law as a positive feature of any lesbian fantasy is instructive.

The denomination of law as nonlesbian reflected in lesbian science fiction is also exhibited in lesbian theory. For example, Sarah Hoagland in *Lesbian Ethics*[11] specifically rejects "justice" as a concept that "exists to sort our competing claims within a system that has as its axis dominance and subordination." As Hoagland conceptualizes lesbianism, because it does not share this axis, concepts like justice are destructive. In a less obvious example, Joyce Treblicot[12] advances three principles that might govern lesbian methodology: speaking only for oneself, not attempting to have others accept one's beliefs, and not accepting any absolutes. Such principles, if adopted by any lesbian legal theory, would mean that there would be no advocates, no advocacy, and no rules. Law as we now know it would be meaningless.

Importantly, however, both Hoagland's and Treblicot's theories, as well as most of the science fictions mentioned above, are concerned with relations among lesbians. The more confrontational definitions contained in the dictionaries are primarily concerned with relationships between lesbians and the dominant culture. Again, this suggests that the positive attributes of any lesbian legal theory will shift according to the participants.

What may be less subject to shifting is the purpose of insuring lesbian survival under the rule of law, as well as the judgment that lesbians and not laws are the theory's focus. The eventual development of our theories will best occur in the context of concrete situations involving lesbians. Perhaps examining the ways in which we survive—and do not survive—under the rule of law will best advance the development of any theory.

REFERENCES

Ruthann Robson, *Embodiments: The Possibilities of Lesbian Legal Theory in Bodies Problematized by Postmodernism and Feminisms*, 1 STANFORD JOURNAL OF LAW, GENDER & SEXUAL ORIENTATION _____ (1992) (forthcoming); Ruthann Robson, *Lesbian Jurisprudence?*, 8 LAW & INEQUALITY: A JOURNAL OF THEORY AND PRACTICE 443 (1990).

ENDNOTES

1. ALEX DETOCQUEVILLE, DEMOCRACY IN AMERICA (originally published in two parts in 1835 and 1840) translated by Henry Reeve (1945). Quote in Chapter XVI, at 280 of Reeve edition.

2. Cheryl Clarke, *Lesbianism, An Act of Resistance,* in THIS BRIDGE CALLED MY BACK: WRITINGS BY RADICAL WOMEN OF COLOR 128 (Cherrie Moraga and Gloria Anzaldúa, eds. Albany: New York: Kitchen Table: Women of Color Press 1983).

3. For further elaboration of this argument, see Ruthann Robson, *Gender and Other Disadvantages: A Review of GENDER AND JUSTICE by Deborah Rhode,* 18 FLORIDA STATE UNIVERSITY LAW REVIEW 883 (1991).

4. An exception to the lack of theoretical stance and inattention to lesbians is the inspirational and impressive work of Rhonda Rivera. Her articles include *Our Straight Laced Judges: The Legal Position of Homosexual Persons in the United States,* 30 HASTINGS LAW JOURNAL 799 (1979); *Queer Law: Sexual Orientation Law in*

the Mid-Eighties, Part I, 10 UNIVERSITY OF DAYTON LAW REVIEW 459 (1985); *Queer Law: Sexual Orientation Law in the Mid-Eighties*, Part II, 11 UNIVERSITY OF DAYTON LAW REVIEW 275 (1986).

5. There are a few hopeful exceptions among gay male legal scholars. The work of Francisco Valdes is especially promising. See, *Queers, Sissies and Tomboys: Notes and Thoughts on the Connectivities of Women and Sexual Minorities* (forthcoming).

6. MONIQUE WITTIG AND SANDE ZEIG, LESBIAN PEOPLES: MATERIALS FOR A DICTIONARY 95-6 (1979).

7. MARY DALY in cahoots with JANE CAPUTI, WEBSTERS' FIRST NEW INTERGALACTIC WICKEDARY OF THE ENGLISH LANGUAGE (Boston: Beacon Press 1987).

8. JOANNA RUSS, THE FEMALE MAN 50 (1975).

9. SANDI HALL, THE WINGWOMEN OF HERA 45-6 (San Francisco: Spinsters Ink 1987).

10. KATHERINE FORREST, DAUGHTERS OF A CORAL DAWN (Tallahassee, Florida: Naiad Press 1984).

11. SARAH LUCIA HOAGLAND, LESBIAN ETHICS (Palo Alto, California: Institute for Lesbian Studies 1988).

12. Joyce Treblicot, *Dyke Methods*, HYPATIA, Summer 1988, reprinted in LESBIAN PHILOSOPHIES AND CULTURES (Jeffner Allen, ed. 1990).

OUTLAWS

2

SEARCHING FOR A PAST

I f lesbians have been insulated from legal history, then I can imagine the predomesticated lesbian living peacefully outside the law. She walks down a path unhampered by statutes, innocent of gallows, fire, and banishment. She is my ancestor outlaw.

She is not my private fantasy. She and her lovers are footnotes of absence in a multitude of scholarly sources. Historians generally believe there were women who committed lesbian acts (even if some believe such women cannot properly be called lesbians), but that such women remained unpunished by the law. Men were routinely executed or otherwise punished for sodomy, but women were safe. Most sources of legal history do not mention lesbians at all, not even those sources ostensibly dealing with women's legal history or homosexual legal history. Where lesbians are included, the emphasis is on the irrelevance of lesbianism in legal history: "Traditionally, European culture had condemned male homosexuality and ignored female homosexuality."[1] Or, less emphatically, "Historically, there is less hostility to lesbianism than to male homosexuality."[2]

It felt nice being safe, even retrospectively.

And I began to build theories around lesbian immunity. I concocted an argument that grounded the inapplicability of any criminal laws to lesbian sexuality. The laws were never meant to apply to us.

We were truly outlaws.

Yet I was also suspicious. In the work of the same commentators who minimized the connection between lesbianism and Anglo-European legal history, as well as in the works of others, I was finding oblique references to historical incidents in which lesbianism and the law had a very real relationship. Lesbians had, in fact, been executed for committing lesbian acts. As I searched further, I noticed I felt rewarded when I found such references. Such is the perversity of the researcher. Real pain, real death, is eclipsed. The research project has a life of its own.

As I looked for references to lesbianism in Anglo-European legal history, I became entangled in the problems of being a historian: the one who decides what counts and what does not. What is the significance of focusing on executions? Does that mean that floggings and banishments are inconsequential? For whom? From what point of view? If I were writing a legal history of murder prosecutions, would I only consider executions? Even a legal history of the death penalty might conclude that more than its implementation is worthy of attention.

The historian as researcher decides whether precontemporary lesbians are more properly found in an unmanageable "morally insane" housemaid, Magdalena Van W., who had "the habit of holding her hands to her genitals at night, and even went so far as to invite her aunt, with whom she shared a bed...and even to try to force her to do it together as man and woman," or in a romantic "friend" who authors elaborate love letters.[3] This essentially class conflict has special resonance for attempts at an Anglo-European legal history of lesbianism. If I choose the writer of love letters as the predecessor, I might easily reach the conclusion that lesbianism was unpunished and unpunishable. If I choose the housemaid, I might conclude that lesbianism was censured by the law, although perhaps under different rubrics, such as "vagrancy" or "moral insanity."

Many of these problems surfaced in my thinking as I considered a famous nineteenth-century British case in which two schoolteachers, Woods and Pirie, sued a student's grandmother, Lady Cumming Gordon, for slander based on accusations of lesbianism.[4] Many scholars rely on this case to show that lesbianism was legally unimaginable in the nineteenth century. The court upheld the action for slander, reasoning in part that the crime of lesbianism had never been known in Britain or Scotland. One judge stated that the consideration of lesbianism is "unparalleled in any court, since the creation of time." The judges, however, also made statements that they would believe the allegations "if well proved," but that the facts lacked coherency. The issue before the court centered on truth as a defense to slander, a topic discussed in its contemporary incarnation in chapter 5. In the Woods/Pirie case, Lady Cumming Gordon had to prove the actual commission of the "infamous crime of *venus nefada*—of unnatural lust—the most infamous of all offenses." The first member of the judiciary to handle any aspect of the case initially refused the possibility (both morally and physically) that any Scotch ladies could act in such a manner. The defense presented a twenty-page list of "Authorities with Regard to the Practise of Tribadism." As to the existence of this crime of *venus nefada*, the judges had differing and often complex and convoluted reactions. There was an initial stated disbelief that this "crime" existed (was physically possible), existed in civilization (Scotland), existed without the right physiology (large clitori, as the jurists racistly assumed belonged to "African women"), existed without the right equipment (certain "tools"), or existed among women such as Woods and Pirie (educated, good families, solid class backgrounds, Christian).

Thus, the rejection of lesbianism was not simplistic, bounded as it was by geography, circumstance, race, class, education, and religion. Further, accompanying the discussion of these factors, there was extensive (often twenty to thirty pages) fact-specific reasoning. The judges evaluated the veracity of witnesses, the probability that the acts occurred where they were said to have occurred rather than someplace else, the state of mind of Woods and Pirie, and the worth of the evidence. While it is clear that some of the judges in this case did express disbelief as to the crime of lesbianism, to imply that the court merely rejected the possibility of such a crime is overly simplistic: not all the judges agreed that lesbian sexual acts did not occur, and even those who did engaged in case-specific reasoning. Reducing the Woods/Pirie case to a simplistic silhouette adds to the erasure of lesbianism in Anglo-European legal history.

In addition, we should be wary of making generalizations about women's sexuality. The Victorian mentality that posited women as passionless (or perhaps, more accurately, posited that women should aspire to passionlessness) was not applicable to all women. Lower-class women were routinely arrested for committing "crimes against chastity" or "lewd and lascivious behavior."[5] Prostitution flourished in both Britain and the United States during this period. The much-accepted argument that homosexuals became a recognized medical/legal category during this period seems to me to be equally applicable to prostitutes. The categorization of *prostitute* is a movement away from the perception that some women supplemented their incomes by sexual services, to a view that some women were reducible to their employment. There is a historical connection, legal and otherwise, between lesbians and prostitutes.[6] It is interesting to consider not only how many lesbians supported themselves by prostitution, but how many lesbian sexual acts were prosecuted as prostitution-related offenses. Perhaps prostitution was an umbrella term for women's sexual transgressions in the same way that *sodomy* was used to condemn male "deviant" sexual acts.

It is a vicious cycle: our assumptions of invisibility and nonexistence become the realities underpinning misconstruction and imperceptibility. Many sources take lesbianism as nonexistent in legal history because lesbians are not at its center. Yet the official version is repeated so often it obscures any other possibility.

As lesbians, we have a stake in a legal history that promises us the safety of those who are not noticed. Nonlesbians also have certain stakes in lesbian invisibility in legal history. For gay men, the diminishment of lesbianism insures that the focus will be on gay male prosecutions and executions for sodomy. As one gay male scholar explains, "One reason for this absence of knowledge [about lesbianism] is the legal situation—the fact that lesbianism was not generally subject to legal sanctions—and thus there were no pillorying scandals to seize the public imagination." Yet some pages later this same scholar alludes to "a series of public pilloryings of lesbians in the 1920's and thereafter."[7] These public punishments of lesbians are not documented further. They remain unworthy of discussion, apparently, because they are not discussed. This construction of lesbians in legal history supports conclusions about the larger culture of lesbianism: "A lesbian subculture did exist, but was a pale version of the male, and even more overwhelmingly upper class."[8]

Lesbianism may not only be diminished, it may be reinterpreted. Feminists who are more interested in gender relations than in lesbianism may thus construe lesbian legal history as having more to do with gender than with lesbian sexuality. Commentaries to the 1721 trial of Catharina Margaretha Linck and Catharina Margaretha Muhlhahn are illustrative.[9]

The trial record relates that Linck, or Lincken as she is also called, disguised herself in men's clothes, gained and lost the gift of prophesy, joined the troops as a musketeer, deserted, reenlisted, vacillated between wearing male and female attire, made flannel, did spinning and printing, again adopted male attire, and went to work for a stocking-maker, where she met the codefendant, Muhlhahn. The two were married in 1717. The trial record also relates the sexual experiences of the women, the abuse by Linck of her lover, the couple's poverty, the discovery of Linck's gender by Muhlhahn's mother, and the "explanations" and "confessions" of both women, perhaps obtained pursuant to torture. Much of the trial record, however, concerns a discussion of the proper punishment to be administered to Linck: being hung with the body burned afterward OR being put to death by the sword OR being burned alive. "It is only fair to determine the penalty according to the seriousness of the crime." The judicial reasoning in this record, like the judicial reasoning in the Woods/Pirie trial— like modern judicial reasoning—is an application by the authorities to the facts of the case. The facts causing the decision-makers the most consternation concerned the evidence of a "leather instrument" used by Linck during sexual acts, thus making it unclear what degree of sodomy (and thus what punishment) should be applicable. That Linck should be put to death was not seriously debated; the legal issue was how to affect this.

Yet lesbian sexuality can be minimalized by attributing it to something above and beyond her lesbianism. For example, one feminist scholar argues that "this case illustrates the true nature of patriarchal outrage, however, which emerges equally from all other comparable examples. Linck's offense was not to have made love to her 'wife,' but to have usurped male attire to do so."[10] In this commentator's view, the real crime is crossdressing or transvestism: the adoption of male attire. Lesbian sexuality is minimalized.

Crossdressing and lesbian sexuality are intertwined. This is neither to contend that all crossdressers are lesbians, nor that all lesbians are crossdressers, either in this century or in previous ones. Yet many lesbian sources attest to the significance of crossdressing to lesbian history, and at least one researcher of crossdressing found "rather unexpectedly" that the study of crossdressing provided "new ideas and insights into the history of female homosexuality."[11]

I do not mean to disparage our efforts to consider the meaning of prohibitions, punishments, or pronouncements about crossdressing, lesbian sexuality, or any other facet of lesbian existence. I believe feminist theories of gender and power are quite appropriate in this context. I also believe that gay male theory and history have much to lend us. Nevertheless, I think we need to question all sublimations of lesbianism into dual-gendered theories. I also think we need to question all comparisons of lesbianism with (male) homosexuality, especially where the results make men the measure of all things and make women's experience "invisible" or "less" or "pale."

I am not arguing that Anglo-European legal history has been preoccupied with lesbianism, or that it has unremittingly devoted its considerable energies over the centuries to eradicating lesbianism. I am, instead, making a claim that lesbianism might not so cavalierly and categorically be relegated to extra-legal status.

Furthermore, if we put lesbians at the center of our theories about lesbians in legal history, then it becomes important whether even a single lesbian was punished for her love for another woman (any woman, including herself). One woman executed for being a lesbian, one woman banished or pilloried or flogged or incarcerated, is not incidental. It is not incidental even if that one lesbian was illiterate or dark-skinned or lower class, even if the "crime" of that one lesbian was prostitution or transvestism or lewdness. The punishment of one lesbian is a matter of great import.

If we put lesbians at the center, references to lesbians in Anglo-European legal history become apparent. From secondary sources, and limited only to the European continents, I found references to a legal history of lesbianism. And that history is not necessarily benign.

Ancient Greece and Rome/The Old and New Testaments

If we rely on fragments of Sappho's writing, ancient Greece apparently accepted lesbian relations. Plato, many people's favorite ancient (gay) philosopher, declares to the contrary that "the crime of male with male, or female with female, is an outrage on nature and a capital surrender to lust of pleasure."[12] Ancient Rome was in accord with this view of lesbian sexuality. A married woman found engaged in any sexual activity with another woman, even mutual caressing, could be tried as an adulteress. Her husband was her executioner. An influential Roman statesman argued that any married woman who engaged in lesbian sexual expression should be put to death as a just penalty for her crime,[13] and a well-known poet urged that all Roman lesbians should lose their property and possibly their lives.[14]

Greek and early Roman proclamations had less influence in Europe than the imperial legislation of Christian Rome. The sixth-century encyclopedic collection of Roman law, *Corpus juris civilis*, served as the basis for canon law (the law of the Christian church) and civil law (both European and English). It provided that those guilty of either adultery or giving themselves up to "works of lewdness with their own sex" were to receive the death penalty. Many ecclesiastical jurists of the Middle Ages revived and researched Roman law, including Cino da Pistoia, who interpreted a Roman edict prohibiting certain sexual transgressions to include "when a woman suffers defilement in surrendering to another woman."[15]

Christian Rome derived much of its law from biblical sources. There is apparently no mention of lesbianism in the Old Testament, only the prohibition against witchcraft and crossdressing.[16] In the New Testament, Paul's Epistle as textualized in Romans 1:26 provides the basis for the condemnation of lesbian sexuality. While the Biblical passage is rather enigmatic, referring to women changing the natural into the unnatural,[17] early Christian commentators unequivocally interpreted it as a condemnation of lesbianism. St. Ambrose (d. 397 A.D.), for example, stated that "God being angry with the human race because of their idolatry, it came about that a woman would desire a woman for the use of foul lust." Another influential Christian theologian, St. John Chrysostom (d. 407 A.D.), preaching on Romans 1:26 at Antioch about 390 A.D., paraphrased the passage by declaring that in Paul's day, "even women again abused women, and not men only," and added that "it is even more shameful that the women should seek this type of intercourse, since they ought to have more modesty than men." In the seventh and eighth centuries, lesbian sexual acts are specifically identified as sins and therefore subject to punishment.[18]

The Middle Ages

The Christian legal tradition continued to accept the Pauline proscription against lesbian sexuality. St. Augustine supposedly declared: "Acts contrary to nature are in truth always illicit, and without a doubt more shameful and foul, which use the Holy Apostle has condemned both in women and in men, meaning them to be understood as more damnable than if they had sinned through the natural use by adultery or fornication." Other authoritative saints reinforced Pauline doctrine condemning lesbian sexuality. Church authorities punished tribadism and any use of the "artificial phallus." Nuns were prohibited from sleeping together. St. Albertus Magnus (1206-1280) included female sodomy among the worst sexual sins. St. Thomas Aquinas (1225-1274), in the influential *Summa Theologia*, adopted the view that lesbianism is included in the vice of sodomy.

Canon law and Catholic moral theology had a very considerable influence in shaping medieval secular law; some Carolingian Kings actually promulgated the canons of various church councils as laws of the realm. One of the most infamous secular laws against lesbian sexual activity is found in the 1260 Code for the district of Orleans, France—*Li Livres di jostice et de plet*. It provided:

22. He who has been proved to be a sodomite must lose his testicles. And if he does it a second time, he must lose his member. And if he does it a third time, he must be burned.
23. A woman who does this shall lose her member each time, and on the third must be burned. (Feme qui le fet doit a chescune foiz perde membre et la tierce doit estre arsse.)[19]

The statute does not explain how the lesbian's loss of her member two times was to be implemented.

Secular jurists during this period also relied upon Roman law to criminalize lesbian sexuality. Two commentators of this school were regularly cited by later authorities to justify the punishment of lesbians. These references were standard until the eighteenth century and could have the force of law. Thus, by using these references it would have been possible to argue for the death penalty for lesbianism even in parts of the continent with no such national or local legislation.

The Renaissance and the Enlightenment

During the European periods known as the Renaissance and the Enlightenment, roughly the fourteenth through eighteenth centuries, secular prohibitions of lesbianism gradually became less intertwined with religious decrees, as well as more explicit. For example, in the Holy Roman Empire under Emperor Charles V (1519-1556), the civil constitution provided that an impurity of "a woman with a woman" merits a sentence of death by burning.[20] A small town near Venice, Italy, adopted a statute in 1574 proscribing sexual relations of "a woman with a woman if they are twelve or more." It mandated the punishment as "she shall be fastened naked to a stake in the street of Locusts and shall remain there all day and night under a reliable guard and the following day shall be burned outside the city."[21] Lodovico Maria Sinistrarik, a Franciscan, attempted to codify punishment for sodomy in *Peccatum Mutum* (1700), but only defined sodomy as the use of an enlarged clitoris to penetrate another woman. He prescribed the appropriate punishment as torture on the rack.[22]

In Spain and Italy, lesbianism could bring the death penalty. Influential jurists from each country developed degrees of punishment dependent on the severity of the crime. Burning was the penalty for the use of any "material instrument," or as an Italian jurist so eloquently expressed it, "introducing some wooden or glass instrument into the belly of another." Refrain from instruments warranted something less than death: beating was apparently popular. If a woman only made overtures to another, then public denouncement was the appropriate penalty. These distinctions, based on male views of sexuality, have considerable and long-lived influence.[23]

Despite this relative explicitness, the commitment to silence remained entrenched. For example, a fifteenth-century rector, Jean Gerson, relied upon Aquinas to conclude that lesbianism was a crime against nature, describing it as a sin in which "women have each other by detestable and horrible means which should not be named or written." This silence extended to secular authorities. Germain Colladon, a famous sixteenth-century jurist, advised Genevan authorities who had no prior experience with lesbian crimes that the death sentence should be read publicly, but that the customary description of the crime should be omitted. Thus, when the execution of a lesbian by drowning—a popular means of execution in Germany and Switzerland—was orchestrated by Colladon in 1568, the official sentence ruminated on blasphemy and fornication, adding only that there was also a "detestable and unnatural crime, which is so ugly that, from horror, it is not named here."[24] Given such silences, it is quite possible that more women were punished for lesbian sexual acts, but that their crimes were unnamed or misnamed in official records.

Nevertheless, throughout Europe during the Renaissance and Enlightenment, there are references to executions and other punishments of women for lesbian sexual acts and crossdressing. In sixteenth-century Spain, two nuns were burned for using "material instruments," while in France, a transvestite was burned for "counterfeit[ing] the office of husband." A case of lesbian sexuality was brought before the parliament of Toulouse in 1553 and another in 1555, while two other women were tried and tortured but eventually acquitted for insufficient evidence. In Germany, a girl was drowned at Speier in 1477 for "lesbian love." In Italy, a woman was hanged in 1580 for "engaging in a lesbian love affair."[25]

Most of the above cases are preserved only by accident. The last mentioned, for example, the hanging in Italy, is recorded in Montaigne's diary. One of the best documented cases, that of a lesbian nun in Renaissance Italy, was found "by chance, while leafing through an inventory of nearly forgotten documents in the State Archive in Florence." The researcher was drawn to the document because it was related to a town about which she was writing, and to its title: "Papers relating to a trial against Sister Benedetta Carlini of Vellano, abbess of the Theatine nuns of Pescia, who pretended to be a mystic, but who was discovered to be a woman of ill repute." The nun's special companion, Bartolemea, testified during the trial about kissing, mutual masturbation, rubbing, and "corruption," being careful to note the lack of material instruments so important to avoid the death penalty. Sister Benedetta Carlini spent the rest of her life—thirty-five years—in prison.[26]

Secular trials of lesbians in the Netherlands have been discovered by Dutch historians researching female transvestism as a "by-product of our more regular historical research." Restricted in scope, their research is a study of 119 cases of women who dressed as men in the Netherlands between 1550 and 1839, mostly through criminal records, judicial archives, and maritime records. The authors posit that cases of crossdressing were treated very differently when the woman had a sexual relationship with another woman; such women could be convicted of a capital offense. In 1606, Maeyken Joosten was tried for sodomy. Joosten had been married for thirteen years and had four children when she fell in love with Bertelmina Wale. Joosten left her husband, traveled to Zeeland, and returned to Leiden dressed as a man. The two women were married in March and they had "sexual contact." By November, Joosten was on trial for sodomy. Despite the demand for the death penalty, she was instead exiled for life.[27]

In another Dutch trial, the jurists similarly debated the death penalty but acted in ways they considered merciful by imposing only whipping and the banishment of one of the women with a corresponding restriction to city limits of the other. Enforced separation was also the penalty in a Dutch trial in 1688, in which the penalty was exile and a prohibition against the women ever living together again. In two other Dutch cases in which women passed as men and married their lovers, women were exiled or banished from the city of Amsterdam.

Based on a murder trial in which two women were arrested for murdering a third in what might be termed a lesbian love triangle, the authors of the Dutch study date 1792 as the beginning of the Dutch public and police recognition of lesbianism in a noncrossdressing context. "This sensational case was followed by some ten other arrests of women in Amsterdam in the next six years, who were accused of dirty caresses of one another. The accused were all very poor, marginal women."[28] Again, the connection between class and criminalization cannot be ignored in the search for a lesbian legal history.

Witchcraft

A discussion of lesbianism in Anglo-European legal history would be incomplete without reference to witchcraft. Like many others, this area also needs to be subjected to a rigorous class analysis. For centuries, secular and religious legal institutions combined their considerable powers for the purpose of legally eradicating witchcraft by punishing its practitioners. Although there are many explanations for this legal phenomenon, most authorities agree that the accused practitioners of witchcraft were predominantly women who were somehow not encompassed by male authority. Such a definition resonates with at least some of the characteristics attributed to modern lesbians. Witchcraft has also been traditionally linked with heresy, an accusation often lodged against males and associated with sodomitical practices. The association of male and female homosexuality with witchcraft is documented in a 1460 tract appearing during the trial of accused witches in France:

> Sometimes indeed indescribable outrages are perpetrated in exchanging women, by order of the presiding devil, by passing on a woman to other women and a man to other men, an abuse against the nature of women by both parties and similarly against the nature of men, or by a woman with a man outside the regular orifice and in another orifice.[29]

Earlier accounts also mention homosexuality and bisexuality. Apparently, the phrase "*femina cum feminus*" was commonplace in witch trials.

One of the most famous trials was that of Joan of Arc, charged with heresy and witchcraft. Generally well-known is Joan of Arc's refusal to marry and her wearing of male attire, including armor. After her capture, the Inquisition focused on her male attire as proof of criminality. Judges also inquired into her relationships with other women, including the woman who Joan lived with after she left her parents, and another woman with whom Joan admitted sleeping for two nights.[30] Other less documented trials include the Italian trial of Maria "la Medica," charged in 1480 with having been a witch for fourteen years, during which time she regularly attended witches' assemblies, copulating with other witches. Maria received the "unusually light" punishment of life imprisonment.[31] In a later case in Ireland, a woman named Florence Newton was brought to trial in 1661 and accused of aggressively kissing and bewitching a young servant woman, Mary Longdon. In 1582, witches in Avignon were condemned by the Inquisition for having committed "actual sodomy and the most unmentionable crime."[32]

The "unmentionable crime" and the vagueness or inapplicability of the term *sodomy* serve to obscure accusations of lesbian sexuality during the trials of the Inquisition. When we remember that the witch defendants were predominantly women, warnings by theologians and Inquisitors that sodomy was a crime connected to witchcraft can be understood within the context of prohibitions against lesbianism.

The Americas

Contemporaneously with the Inquisition's subjugation of witchcraft by legal means, the conquistadors and other European colonists were quelling the lesbian sexuality they found among the native peoples of the new world. The indigenous peoples of the Americas were not monolithic in culture or custom. There are references to a respected tradition of lesbianism and male homosexuality among tribal peoples; there is also mention of laws among the Aztecs and "pre-Conquest Mexicans" that mandate the death penalty for lesbianism. As Judy Grahn notes, however, "Gay people were often the first Indians killed...even when tribes were tolerated by the white people, their Gay people were mocked and persecuted to the point of changing their behavior for the safety of their people." One missionary details the questions a priest should ask his Indian penitents during confession as including, "Woman with woman, have you acted as if you were a man?" Other missionaries likewise inquired into lesbian sexuality.[33]

Like Catholic missionaries, the Protestants also sought to suppress lesbian sexual acts within their jurisdictions. In 1636, Rev. John Cotton prepared, upon request from the General Court of Massachusetts, legislation for the colony. Cotton included lesbianism— "woman with woman"—in his capital offense of sodomy, but this legislation was not adopted. The Governor of the Massachusetts Bay Colony wrote to Plymouth theologians soon thereafter requesting an opinion concerning "what sodomitical acts" were to be punished by death. At least one theologian, the Rev. Charles Chauncy, who later became president of Harvard University, included "women with women" as a capital offense. The recorded punishments for lesbian sexual acts in Massachusetts at that time, however, were apparently not capital.

The published body of laws in the New Haven Colony generally followed the laws of the Massachusetts Bay Colony, but departed by specifically mandating the death penalty for lesbian sexual acts. In Virginia, a law authored by Thomas Jefferson arguably proscribed lesbianism by providing that "Whosoever shall be guilty of Rape, Polygamy, or Sodomy with a man or woman shall be punished, if a man, by castration, if a woman, by cutting thro' the cartilage of her nose a hole of one half inch in diameter in the least." Whether the Connecticut and Virginia laws acted as effective deterrents, whether such laws remained unenforced, whether prosecution records were not kept or were destroyed or have not yet been located, is unclear. What does seem clear is that America's early legal history of lesbianism cannot be said to be one of total neglect.[34]

Modern Lesbian Legal History

The belief that lesbianism is legally unimaginable permeates consideration of modern lesbian legal history. For example, descendants of Germain Colladon's strategy of silence appear in the British Parliament. Faced with a 1921 amendment to a British bill seeking to penalize any act "of gross indecency between female persons," the members of parliament voted against it. If we consider this in the context of the legal unimaginability of lesbianism, such a piece of legal history is easily assimilated. Yet a different perspective is provided by Sheila Jeffreys in her book, *The Spinster and Her Enemies*. Quoting from debates by the members of Parliament (MP), she suggests that the choice to ignore lesbianism was a deliberate one selected as the best method for eradicating "perverts": the death penalty would "stamp them out," and locking them up as lunatics would "get rid of them," but ignoring them was best because "these cases are self-exterminating." The MPs explicitly recognized the danger of lesbianism: it caused the "destruction" of the Greek civilization and the "downfall" of the Roman Empire; it could cause "our race to decline"; and it would cause the sexual unavailability of women to men ("any woman who engages in this vice will have nothing whatsoever to do with the other sex").[35] A decision by lawmakers that the danger of mentioning an act outweighs the danger of not criminalizing that act rightly belongs in the annals of legal history.

Another example is the fate of lesbians under the Third Reich, a government with a plethora of laws and legal codes. While lesbianism is usually officially ignored, at least one scholar researching the treatment of male homosexuals recounts that although paragraph 175 of the Nazi Code banning homosexual acts did not encompass women (despite the best efforts of the Nazi attorney who provided many of the ideological underpinnings for the laws against homosexuality), there were nevertheless persecutions of lesbians: "some SS officers had arrested and sentenced lesbians" for treason, sent them to a prisoner of war camp, and other prisoners of war were promised a bottle of schnapps for each lesbian they "penetrated."[36] While lesbians may not have been wearing the pink triangle of the homosexuals, as lesbian chronicler Joan Nestle suggests, they may well have worn the black triangle of the asocials,[37] as did prostitutes.

Today as Legal History

As we make legal history today, we continue to perpetuate the mythology of lesbianism as irrelevant in legal discourse. Lesbianism remains virtually unmentioned (see chapter 5) in the numerous discussions of the 1986 United States Supreme Court case *Bowers v. Hardwick*, in which the Court rejected the constitutional challenge to Georgia's sodomy law by a gay man. In a few commentaries, lesbianism is alluded to, usually by a citation to the Georgia case which had previously held that the terms of the statute did not apply to acts between women. What is not mentioned is the speed with which the statute was amended to make clear the criminalization of lesbian sexuality. Or lesbianism is referred to in conjunction with a discussion of heterosexual sodomy, as if both lesbianism and heterosexuality were derivations of homosexuality.

The next chapter discusses the current legal text of lesbian sexuality, putting lesbians at the center of the analysis of laws that might relate to lesbians. But we must continue to recover, discover, and uncover lesbianism in legal history. Lesbianism is not the safe hollow in Anglo-European legal history that I once believed. And while I self-consciously limited this text to Anglo-European legal history, even within that restriction I omitted at least the entire continent of Australia. One can argue that the limit itself is rather indefensible. What about lesbianism in Chinese legal history? In Egyptian, Nigerian, Assyrian legal histories? I can no longer, in good conscience, accept an answer that says there is nothing to say. There are continents and centuries in which lesbians lived their daily lives in interaction with legal systems. That is a part of our legal history. As is a single lesbian who suffered under the rule of law for her lesbian choices, even if that one lesbian lived long ago, or was poor, or worked as a prostitute, or dressed as a man. Even if that one lesbian was not executed, but was "only" banished and forbidden to live with her lover, ever again.

REFERENCES

Ruthann Robson, *Lesbianism in Anglo-European Legal History*, 5 WISCONSIN WOMEN'S LAW JOURNAL 1 (1990).

ENDNOTES

1. B. ANDERSON AND J. ZINSSER, A HISTORY OF THEIR OWN: WOMEN IN EUROPE FROM PREHISTORY TO THE PRESENT 221 (Volume II 1988).

2. VERN BULLOUGH, HOMOSEXUALITY: A HISTORY 117 (1979). Unlike many other writers on homosexuality, however, Bullough devotes an entire chapter to lesbianism in this book. He has been similarly inclusive in his other works.

3. Compare Miriam Everard, *Lesbian History: A History of Change and Disparity*, 12 JOURNAL OF HOMOSEXUALITY 123, 129-30 (1986) with Lillian Faderman, *A Response to Miriam Everard's "Lesbian History: A History of Change and Disparity,"* 15 J. HOMOSEXUALITY 137 (1988).

4. MISS MARIANNE WOODS AND MISS JANE PIRIE AGAINST DAME HELEN GORDON CUMMING (Arno Press 1975).

5. JOHN D'EMILIO AND ESTELLE B. FREEDMAN, INTIMATE MATTERS: A HISTORY OF SEXUALITY IN AMERICA 57 (1988).

6. See generally, Joan Nestle, *Lesbians and Prostitutes: An Historical Sisterhood*, reprinted in JOAN NESTLE, A RESTRICTED COUNTRY 157 (Ithaca, New York: Firebrand Books 1987).

See also, DAVID E. GREENBERG, THE CONSTRUCTION OF HOMOSEXUALITY 321 (1988) (In the early years of the eighteenth century in France, "tribades were sometimes detained by the police or through lettres de cachet as prostitutes were"); A. F. IDE, LOVING WOMEN 53 (1985) (lesbians in ancient Rome "were shunned by the upper class" and were "frequently forced due to economics to register as prostitutes to be able to earn a living."); C. VAN CASSELAER, LOT'S WIFE: LESBIAN PARIS, 1890-1914 at 24 (1986) ("In 1824, brothel keepers had been expressly forbidden 'to allow their girls to sleep two to the same bed; those who are found in bed together during inspection visits can be punished with several days in prison; free lance girls who are found in the same way can be dealt with in the same severe manner. . . . Also the license was taken away from one madam because she was surprised in bed with another woman.' " These regulations "remained in force for most of the nineteenth century.").

7. JEFFREY WEEKS, COMING OUT: A HISTORY OF HOMOSEXUALITY IN BRITAIN FROM THE 19TH CENTURY 95 (1979).

8. *Id.* at 87.

9. Translated by Brigitte Erickson, *A Lesbian Execution in Germany, 1721: The Trial Records*, 6 JOURNAL OF HOMOSEXUALITY 27 (1980) reprinted in THE GAY PAST: A COLLECTION OF HISTORICAL ESSAYS (eds. Licata and Petersen 1985).

The trial is discussed in Louis Crompton, *The Myth of Lesbian Impunity*, 6 JOURNAL OF HOMOSEXUALITY 11 (1981), also reprinted in THE GAY PAST. Crompton's essay remains an isolated classic to which I am enormously indebted.

10. ROSALIND MILES, THE WOMEN'S HISTORY OF THE WORLD 219 (1989).

11. R. DEKKER AND L. VAN DE POL, THE TRADITION OF FEMALE TRANS-VESTISM IN EARLY MODERN EUROPE 69 (1989) (hereinafter TRANS-VESTISM).

12. Plato, *Laws I*, contained in THE COLLECTED DIALOGUES OF PLATO, LAWS I, 636c at 1237 (1961 ed. edited by E. Hamilton & H. Cairns).

13. A. IDE, LOVING WOMEN: A STUDY OF LESBIANISM TO 500 CE 49 (1985) citing The Elder Seneca 1.2.23.

14. *Id.* at 50, 62.

15. Vern Bullough, *supra* note 2, at 31-32.

16. The precise meaning of the prohibition against witchcraft is interesting to consider in light of its sexual context:

> 16. And if a man entice a maid that is not bethroed, and lie with her, he shall surely endow her to be his wife.
> 17. If her father utterly refuse to give her unto him, he shall pay money according to the dowry of virgins.
> 18. Thou shalt not suffer a witch to live.
> 19. Whosoever lieth with a beast shall be put to death.

Exodus 22: 16-19. Compare Deuteronomy 18: 9-12 (describing as an abomination any one who uses divination, or an observer of times, or enchanter, or witch, or charmer, or wizard).

> A woman shall not wear that which pertaineth unto a man, neither shall a man put on a woman's garment, for all that do so are abomination unto the Lord thy God.

Deuteronomy 22:5

17. "God gave them up into vile affections: for even their women did change the natural use into that which is against nature." Romans 1:26.

18. DERRICK BAILEY, HOMOSEXUALITY AND THE WESTERN CHRISTIAN TRADITION (1955); JUDITH BROWN, IMMODEST ACTS 167 (1986); H.M. HYDE, THE LOVE THAT DARED NOT SPEAK ITS NAME 31 (1970); Crompton, *supra* note 9 at 14.

19. Crompton, *supra* note 9 at 13; Bailey, *supra* note 18 at 142.

20. LILLIAN FADERMAN, SURPASSING THE LOVE OF MEN 49 (1980) (citing Hirschfield, Magnus, DIE HOMOSEXUALITAT DED MANNES UND DES WEIBES (Berlin: Louis Marcus, 822 (1925)).

21. Crompton, *supra* note 9 at 18.

22. Faderman, *supra* note 20 at 35; n.13 at 418. Presumption of this type of lesbian activity if two women accused of sleeping together and upon physical examination one has what is considered a "sufficiently large clitoris" and the women have known to lay with one another.

23. Brown, *supra* note 18 at 14; Crompton, *supra* note 9 at 19.

24. Monter, *Sodomy and Heresy in Early Modern Switzerland*, 6 JOURNAL OF HOMOSEXUALITY 41 (1980/1). See also, J. Brown *supra* note 18 at 19-20, 173n.61 citing Monter, *La Sodomie a l'epoque moderne en Suisse romande*, ANNALES, E.S.C. 1029 (1974). Males convicted of sodomy had their crimes read aloud.

25. Crompton, *supra* note 9 at 17; Faderman, *supra* note 20 at 51; J. Brown, *supra* note 18 at 165n.5.

26. J. Brown, *supra* note 18 at 3.

27. TRANSVESTISM, *supra* note 11 at 1-4.

28. *Id.*

29. ARTHUR EVANS, WITCHCRAFT AND THE GAY COUNTERCULTURE 76 (1978) citing Robbins, Encyclopedia of Witchcraft and Demonology 468 (1959).

30. *Id.* at 6.

31. J.B. RUSSELL, WITCHCRAFT IN THE MIDDLE AGES 260, 261 (1972).

32. Evans, *supra* note 29 at 168.

33. JUDY GRAHN, ANOTHER MOTHER TONGUE 49-72 (1984); JONATHAN KATZ, GAY AMERICAN HISTORY: A DOCUMENTARY 283-87 (1976); Paula Gunn Allen, *Lesbians in American Indian Cultures*, 7 CONDITIONS 67 (1981) reprinted in *A Retrospective:* 16 CONDITIONS 84 (1989).

34. Oaks, *Defining Sodomy in Seventeenth Century Massachusetts,* 6 JOURNAL OF HOMOSEXUALITY 79, 81 (1980/1); J. Katz, *supra* note 33 at 85.

35. SHEILA JEFFREYS, THE SPINSTER AND HER ENEMIES 114 (1985).

36. RICHARD PLANT, THE PINK TRIANGLE 114 (1986). Plant provides other examples of the "arbitrary punishment of real or presumed lesbian relationships" and refers to interviews being conducted by Ilse Kokula, a Berlin social worker and journalist with lesbian survivors of Hitler's regime.

37. Joan Nestle, *supra* note 6 at 174.

3

CRIMES OF LESBIAN SEX

About half the jurisdictions in the United States have statutes that criminalize lesbian sexual expressions, and virtually every state has had a statute as recently as 1968 that would imprison someone for lesbian sexual expression. Many of us tend to dismiss such statutes as not really applicable to us: the statutes are anachronisms; the statutes are law in states that are conservative; the statutes are meant to apply to acts other than what we do; the statutes are directed at other sorts of lesbians. Rarely do we know what these statutes actually say. Yet these statutes are the legal text of lesbian sexuality. Enacted and codified, interpreted and applied, these statutes are the legislative pronouncements and judicial discourse on the subject of who we are sexually. Thus, in any discussions of the law by lesbians, and in any lesbian legal theory, we need to examine these statutes and their judicial interpretations.

The statutes are generally referred to as sodomy statutes and usually discussed in terms of gay male sexuality. Centering lesbian concerns, I instead refer to the statutes as the lesbian sex statutes. This does not mean, however, that I concede the statutes always or only apply to lesbian sexuality. The statutes, individually and collectively, are idiosyncratic in their application to various expressions of lesbian sexuality.

The existing lesbian sex statutes employ what I consider to be three different strategies to describe that which they criminalize: oral/anal, natural, and gender specificity. These strategies may overlap within a given statute, or a state may have a statutory scheme that utilizes more than one.

What I am calling the oral/anal strategy usually prohibits any sexual contact between the sex organs (described also as genitals) of one person, and the mouth or anus of another. These statutes are anatomically specific to a certain extent, but they also target what is generally considered sodomy—sexual contact between a man's penis and an anus, or sexual contact between a man's penis and a mouth, also called fellatio. A few states broaden this strategy by also including objects, fingers, and body parts as prohibited penetrators of sexual organs.

The second strategy relies on so-called natural understandings for its meaning. Statutes criminalize "the crime against nature," or the "abominable and detestable crime against nature," or reversing the adjectives, "the detestable and abominable crime against nature," or "the infamous crime against nature." This strategy, standing alone, is amazingly insufficient to advise anyone of any acts that are within the prohibition. Nevertheless, many courts—including the United States Supreme Court—have upheld such statutes from constitutional vagueness attacks by reasoning that our common understanding includes knowledge of what such statutes prohibit, or that even if common knowledge is not so definite, judges interpreting the statute can rely on established legal understandings.[1] The failure to name what is prohibited, reminiscent of the tactics of the sixteenth century jurist Germain Colladon and the 1920s members of British Parliament discussed in the last chapter, is inherent in statutes that rely on natural understandings. If one wanted to learn specifics about lesbian sexuality, or about any type of sexuality, the natural strategy statutes would definitely not be the place to go.

The third strategy relies on gender specificity for meaning. Often, although not always, gender specificity targets persons of the same sex, and often, although again not always, this strategy is combined with either the oral/anal or the natural strategies. Interestingly, the specificity of gender is also usually coupled with a prohibition against sexual contact with animals. Statutes within this strategy can be some of the broadest in terms of criminalizing lesbian sexual expressions, especially if such statutes criminalize sexual contact between persons of the same sex.

There are not many reported cases—cases which have been through an appeal process and are printed in official state reporters—in which any of these statutes have been applied to consensual activity, and even fewer of those cases involve adult women. There are a few cases, however, and in one a 1968 Michigan appellate court upheld the conviction and prison sentence of one and one-half to five years in the Detroit House of Corrections based on facts it described as follows:

> Defendant [Julie Livermore] visited Mrs. Carolyn French at the public camping grounds at Sunrise Lake in Osceola county, Michigan. Mrs. French had been tent-camping with her 4 children at Sunrise Lake for several days.
>
> About 9 p.m. that same evening, defendant and Mrs. French were observed by complainant Jerry Branch and others, to be in close bodily contact with each other, which continued for approximately one hour. The defendant and Mrs. French then entered the latter's tent.
>
> Later, on receiving a complaint, Troopers. . .of the Michigan state police, proceeded to the Sunrise Lake camping ground. They arrived there about midnight, talked to the complainant and others and then stood within 15 feet of the French tent. Obscene language and conversation indicative of sexual conduct occurring between 2 female persons was overheard by the troopers for about 10 minutes. From the information received from complainant, the obscene language and conversation, and noises overheard, the troopers took action in the belief that a felony had been committed or was being committed at that time. They approached the tent, identified themselves and requested admittance; there was no reply; the troopers unzipped the outer flap, and aided by a flashlight observed a cot located directly in front of the doorway on which defendant and Mrs. French were lying, partially covered by a blanket; the two females were advised that they were under arrest and after taking several flash pictures the troopers permitted them to dress in private.[2]

No matter the wording of any particular statute, each statute has the capacity to be interpreted to include two women "lying, partially covered by a blanket" who have been overheard engaged in "obscene language and conversation indicative of sexual conduct." This case indicates the horrific potential that all the statutes possess.

The case is also typical in its lack of specificity. A lesbian sex statute may explicitly exempt the state from a requirement that it specify the acts alleged to be criminal.[3] Judicial opinions often decline to relate the actual acts that constitute the crime.[4] When described at all, lesbian sexuality is described in clinical terms, or with reference to male sexuality, or simply as unnatural, deviant, or sexual. The few factual descriptions are not provided by lesbians, but by lawyers and judges interpreting lesbian sexual activity. Similarly, I think it is a fairly safe assumption, given the continuing infrequency of women legislators, that none of the lesbian sex statutes was authored by a lesbian. Lesbians are at the margins of the legal text of our own sexuality. One way to center lesbians is to engage in a specific and contextualized analysis of the legal interpretations of some common lesbian sexual activities as described from a lesbian point of view.

The main character, and sometimes narrator, of Judith McDaniel's recent novel *Just Say Yes* is the twenty-six-year-old lesbian, Lindsey.[5] She is waitressing in Provincetown for the summer, wondering about her life, and experiencing sexual encounters. The following five passages and their legal analyses reveal how our sexual practices violate—and fail to violate—the various laws in various states in idiosyncratic ways.

1.

> *Ra's hands spread the lips of her cunt wide and her voice invited Lindsey to stroke the clitoris, move slowly up to the shell-pink little button hiding under the fleshy hood. . . . Letting her one hand follow Ra's rhythm, Lindsey began to stroke lightly with her other, up the belly first, then to the bottom cup of one breast, then the other. . . . Suddenly Ra's knees jerked, and Lindsey felt the orgasm starting under her fingers. She rubbed Ra's clitoris until she was sure she'd gone over the edge, then let her fingers burrow into Ra's wet center and catch at the waves of orgasm pulsing down her abdomen.*

Whether Lindsey and Ra are guilty of criminal conduct depends, in part, upon which strategy a state uses in its lesbian sex statute(s). However, in all states that might criminalize this encounter—as well as any other lesbian encounter—if one party is guilty, then both are guilty, assuming consent. The state can choose to prosecute only one person, which will assist the state in proving its case if the other person cooperates. Consent will not be a defense.

In states that employ only the oral/anal strategy, the sexual encounter between Lindsey and Ra is not within the statute. Thus, in Alabama, Kentucky, Georgia, and Utah, Lindsey has not committed any crime. Whether Lindsey's acts violate statutes dedicated to the natural strategy depends on whether the courts in the particular state have chosen to interpret the statute narrowly (to prohibit only oral/anal sexual activity) or broadly (to "cover the entire field of unnatural acts," as a Nevada court expressed it). In Idaho, committed to a broad interpretation by prior case law, if a court found Lindsey's acts within the statute, the mandatory minimum sentence would be five years; since no maximum sentence is listed, it could legally be life imprisonment.

Lindsey's acts are most likely to violate the statutes that target not acts, but actors—persons of the same gender. In Louisiana, for example, the "use of the genital organ of one of the offenders" is sufficient to constitute the crime if both parties are of the same sex. And in Missouri, "any sexual act involving the genitals of one person and the mouth, tongue, hand, or anus of another person" is a crime if the parties are of the same sex. In Arkansas, the statute combines anatomical specificity with gender specificity to criminalize penetration of the vagina or anus by any body member of a person of the same sex. Lindsey's fingers surely qualify as body members, but how does their "burrowing" translate into the legally required penetration? Arkansas' penetration requirement is not unique, and statutes that resort to any of the three strategies often include a penetration requirement either in the statute itself or in judicial interpretations of the statute. But even if *burrow* means legal penetration, Lindsey might not be a criminal in Texas, where the recently enacted statute criminalizes deviate sexual intercourse defined as activities between persons of the same sex in which "the penetration of the genitals or the anus of another person with an object" occurs. In Texas, then, if Lindsey had burrowed with a dildo, she would violate the statute, but the question remains as to whether her fingers qualify as an object. While our everyday understanding of the word *object* might be limited to the inanimate, a Texas court could decide to give effect to the intention of the legislature. Confronted with Lindsey and Ra, a court might attempt to decide whether Texas legislators intended to include fingers as objects, or whether criminalizing Lindsey and Ra's activities had been their intention.

2.

> *Ra knelt, and Lindsey felt her shoulders between her knees, her tongue probing as her fingers parted the lips of Lindsey's vagina. Ra sucked and nibbled, swallowed from Lindsey's smooth wetness, then moved her tongue hard against Lindsey's clitoris, pushing, circling, then pushing again until an orgasm pulsed out of Lindsey's toes, pushing up to her thighs, swelling her cunt, and throbbing finally into her uterus.*

In states that rely upon the oral/anal strategy in their lesbian sex statutes, Ra's tongue on Lindsey's clitoris is a crime. Lindsey and Ra could be jailed for twenty years in Georgia, five years in Virginia, one year in Alabama and Kentucky, and six months in Utah. The absence of anal sex will not help Lindsey and Ra, unless they are in the California prison system, which only criminalizes anal penetration by a penis by inmates, and possibly if they are in South Carolina, which only criminalizes the undefined act of "buggery."[6]

One of the more interesting states in which to consider the placement of Ra's tongue is Kansas. Kansas criminalizes what it calls sodomy between persons of the same sex, but the statute explicitly defines sodomy as "oral-anal copulation, including oral-genital stimulation between the tongue of a male and the genital area of a female." The "including" in the Kansas statute, added by a 1990 amendment, is an excluding of female tongues. At least this is the interpretation of authoritative comments to the statutes, as well as of the state's highest court. In Kansas, Ra and Lindsey do not violate the proscription against oral sex.

The Kansas situation is not historically unique. A 1939 Georgia court held that lesbian cunnilingus was not a crime under the statute that prohibited the "carnal knowledge and connection against the order of nature, by man with man, or in the same unnatural manner with woman." The court concluded that "man" was the exclusive actor, and held the unspecified acts between two women were excluded even though they were "just as loathsome."[7] The Georgia legislature subsequently amended the statute to rely on the oral/anal strategy and eliminate any gender references.

Courts in other states, however, have found lesbian cunnilingus clearly illegal. Under Louisiana's prior crime against nature statute (since amended to reflect the oral/anal strategy), the women who participated in "oral copulation by and between both of the accused" had their convictions of thirty months in prison affirmed.[8] In

Oklahoma, under a crime against nature statute still in effect, in a case involving interracial lesbian (and heterosexual) acts, the court had no difficulty accepting the proposition that the statute's reference to "mankind" included both male and female and that "copulation per os between two females" was criminal.[9] Yet because Oklahoma's statutory scheme also includes a requirement of "penetration, however slight" an appellate court—despite its expressed disagreement with the penetration requirement—reversed the conviction of a woman who admitted performing cunnilingus on another female because the prosecutor "made no effort to introduce any evidence, either direct or circumstantial, proving the essential element of penetration."[10] What penetration means—and what it is that must be penetrated—is unclear. Is Ra's tongue against Lindsey's clitoris penetration?

3.

> *They didn't undress, and there seemed to be little urgency in their movements at first, just a gentle rocking of bodies entwined, interlocked in the right way. Sindar had slipped her hard, round thigh between Lindsey's legs, brought it right up against the rough seam of her pants crotch, and began to move up and down, up and down. Mesmerized, Lindsey lay quietly at first, one hand holding Sindar's shoulder as she rocked, the other resting on the back of her head, feeling the tightly braided dreads, pressing Sindar's mouth tight into her own. . . . Together they rocked, feeling the tension build, the wetness seep through the cloth. . . . Lindsey felt Sindar's orgasm begin when her rhythm changed, became more urgent, forceful, and her faster thrusts brought Lindsey over the edge too, let her gasp with relief as she felt the orgasm ripple up her thighs and into her belly.*

The clinical term for Lindsey and Sindar's lovemaking is *tribadism*, and as an activity that does not include oral/anal contact with sexual organs, or any penetration, it is criminalized only by the most broadly worded statutes that would also criminalize Lindsey's previously discussed interactions with Ra. Among the broadest of these statutes are ones that clearly target same-sex activities. For example, Montana's criminalization of "deviate sexual intercourse" includes "any touching of the sexual or other intimate parts of another [of the same sex] for the purposes of arousing or gratifying the sexual desire of either party." If the touchings between Lindsey and Sindar are intended to sexually arouse or gratify either of them, they are guilty in Montana and could be sentenced to ten years. Michigan's statute prohibiting gross indecency between women—the statute under which Julie Livermore was convicted because of her activities at the campground with Carolyn French—is also sufficiently broad to allow a conviction of Lindsey and Sindar, as well as many lesbians at the annual Michigan Women's Music Festival.

Vague statutes employing the natural strategy that do not incorporate gender specificity might also be broad enough to subject Lindsey and Sindar to criminal sanctions. Arizona's statute prohibiting "lewd and lascivious acts" committed in an "unnatural manner" has been specifically stated to apply to acts between consenting adults by Arizona's highest court. Florida has a statute similar to Arizona's, but Florida's highest court has added qualifiers to the statute such as "open and gross" and "extremely indecent." The Florida court thus reversed the conviction of a male waiter in a gay bar who fondled a fully clothed patron, and if they were in Florida, Lindsey and Sindar's clothing might serve to immunize them from conviction and prison.

4.

> *Carol was leading the way now, walking toward the end of the pier. . . . Suddenly, Carol did what she had been doing all week in the freedom of this new environment—she threw her natural caution into the breeze blowing off the ocean and put her arms around Lindsey. Lindsey's lips were waiting. . . . They kissed slowly at first, lips exploring the contours of a face, tasting the skin, breathing in the scent of a new person. Once again her bare thighs were touching Carol's. She began to explore the velvet-smooth skin under Carol's blouse. . . . Her fingers traced the length of Carol's spine, up from the waist to the back of her neck, beneath the shorts to her tailbone, to her firm ass.*
>
> *"Oh, my." Carol moved away from the kiss and took a deep breath.*

Carol and Lindsey are kissing and touching on a public pier, and although each of the previous three scenes also took place in public in Judith McDaniel's novel, I analyzed them as if they occurred behind the proverbial drapes-drawn locked-door bedroom. We need to reconsider privacy, and the next chapter discusses this legal concept in some detail. In the context of lesbian sex statutes, lesbian sex in public—or in any place with a window or other indication that might be interpreted to be less than absolutely private—is subject to being criminalized as indecent exposure, public lewdness, or open and gross lewdness.

Every state in the United States has some sort of statute that prohibits public lesbian sexual expressions. Many of these statutes are aimed at "flashers," and thus target exposure of the genitals in public in a manner likely to be observed. So limited, the statutes would not criminalize Lindsey and Carol's activities on the pier, although Lindsey's prior acts with Ra on that same pier would be criminalized. However, even relatively benign statutes enacted in states that do not have specific lesbian sex statutes contain words that could be interpreted to criminalize Lindsey and Carol. New Jersey prohibits any "flagrantly lewd and offensive act." New York prohibits any "lewd act." New Mexico criminalizes exposure of the breasts. And in Vermont, "open and gross lewdness and lascivious behavior" is a crime that can provoke a five-year prison sentence.

5.

> *I was learning real quick that arguing with a lawyer can take a lot of time and preparation. I let it drop for then because we were climbing those narrow steps again, Carol ahead, me behind. I put both hands under her ass as she climbed. "I don't know about legal definitions," I told her, "but I'd be glad to show you in person what I think a lesbian is."*

That Lindsey's new lover is an attorney with the public defender's office might be convenient should Lindsey be arrested for the crime of solicitation to violate a lesbian sex statute. Soliciting a person to commit a crime is an independent offense in many jurisdictions. Solicitation is often used to prosecute what the state considers prostitution, but there need not be a mention of money if the act solicited is lesbian sex. In the District of Columbia, for example, it is illegal "for any person to invite, entice, persuade, or address for the purpose of inviting, enticing, or persuading" any person for an "immoral or lewd purpose." The D.C. courts have expressly limited "immoral and lewd" to acts encompassed by their sodomy statute, which uses the oral/anal strategy to criminalize lesbian sex. The courts have rejected free speech challenges to this criminal solicitation statute and have also held that the solicitation need not occur in a public place. So, depending on whether or not Lindsey thinks oral sex would demonstrate "what a lesbian is," she could be subject to a $300 fine. And for her second of-

fense, perhaps inviting Carol over the next day with a similar promise, Lindsey is subject to another $300 fine and ten days in jail. And
for every invitation, enticement, or persuasion thereafter, Lindsey is
subject to an additional $300 fine and ninety days in jail.

As the crimes of Lindsey, Carol, Sindar, and Ra demonstrate,
lesbian sexual expressions and various lesbian sex statutes have a
rather idiosyncratic relationship. Cunnilingus between women is not
criminal in Kansas, but should the tongue stray toward the anus and
any "penetration, however slight" occur, then it is a crime with a sentence of six months in prison. A finger inside a lesbian lover is illegal
in Missouri; a dildo is legal. But not in Texas, where dildo use will be
a criminal act and fingers, unless they are objects, are legal. Such disparities are partially explained by the commitment to male sexuality
embedded in the statutes. While the statutes seek to criminalize lesbian sex—I cannot think of any applicable statute that actually intends
to exclude lesbianism from sexual deviancy—the attempted criminalization occurs within a frame of reference that centers male sexuality.

There are several lesbian theorists, most notably Marilyn Frye,
arguing that *sex* is a term not applicable to lesbians. Frye's view is supported by the haphazard manner in which the lesbian sex statutes,
considered as a whole, apply to lesbians. When we consider statutes
or interpretations that require penetration, for example, it does not
mean that lesbians have a uniform disdain or appreciation for penetration—whatever penetration means—but that penetration is not
definitional of lesbian sex. Whatever our personal preferences, I think
most of us would describe both Lindsey's interactions with Ra and
with Sindar as "sex," and most of us would not consider one encounter
as "less sex" than any other from Lindsey's point of view. The lesbian
sex statutes and their judicial constructions centralize male sexuality,
however, not lesbian sexuality.

While I am certainly not advocating that all statutes be broadened to include all lesbian relating, the statutes and their interpretations do constitute the legal text of our sexuality, and we need to
think about the absences and rationales in that text. The refusal to explicitly state the acts criminalized is a violence. This absence is violent
not only because if one wished to comply with the law (as the law assumes), one would need to avoid a wide spectrum of activities, but
also because the only references to our sexuality within the legal text
are constructed around profound absences. The rationales in the text
are also violent. Although it is a relief in some ways to know that in
Kansas my tongue on another lesbian's clitoris is legal, this relief is tem-

pered by its rationale: my tongue is somehow less sexual because it shares a body with a clitoris instead of a penis. There is a random violence inherent in determinations of my criminal culpability based upon how deep my tongue penetrates, whether I use my tongue or my fingers, my fingers or an object, whether I eroticize a lover's clitoris, her anus, or her mouth, whether we are clothed or inside or in what state we happen to find ourselves. There is also a violence in the legal text of our sexuality that would describe any activities within our lovemaking as "deviate," as "perverted," as "unnatural," or even with reference to words like *intercourse* or *copulation*.

The violence of the lesbian sex statutes is the violence of propaganda, the propaganda of nonlesbianism. Because the statutes are rarely enforced—a rarity that insulates them from being challenged or attracting interest—we are tempted to think of the lesbian sex statutes as ineffectual attempts at brainwashing. Yet as propaganda they are effective, not because they prevent us from engaging in lesbian activity, but because they perpetuate violence upon our lesbian survival. They negatively affect our daily survival as support for legal determinations that tolerate discrimination against us, that remove our children from us, as threats that regulate our choices about being open with our sexuality.

The rules of law that are the lesbian sex statutes domesticate us. They are the supporting legal text for any feelings any of us might have that our sexuality is wrong. These laws domesticate us with their paradoxical message: our sexuality is not worthy of inclusion within any legal text; our sexuality is worthy only of being criminalized. It is a violence that may seem intangible, but it is ultimately supported by very tangible people like police, prosecutors, judges, and prison guards. When we appeal to the law as lesbians, we appeal to a legal text that has historically criminalized us and continues to do so.

REFERENCES

Ruthann Robson, *The Legal Text of Lesbian Sex,* (forthcoming).

List of Statutes

State	Citation	Title
Alabama	Ala. Code §13A-6-65	Sexual Misconduct
	§13A-6-60(2)	Deviate Sexual Intercourse
	§13A-6-64	Sodomy
Arizona	Ariz. Rev. Stat. §13-1411	Crime against nature
Arkansas	Ark. Stat. §5-14-122	Sodomy
California	Cal. Penal Code §286(e)	Sodomy [prisoners only]
District of	D.C. Code §22-3502	Sodomy
Columbia	D.C. Code §22-2701	Inviting for purposes of prostitution [and sodomy] prohibited
Georgia	Ga. Code §16-6-2	Sodomy; aggravated sodomy
Florida	Fla. Stat. §800.02	Unnatural and lascivious act
Idaho	Idaho Code §18-6605	Crime against nature
Kansas	Kan. Stat. §21-3505	Criminal sodomy
Kentucky	Ky. Rev. Stat. §510.100	Sodomy in the fourth degree
Louisiana	La. Rev. Stat. §89	Crime against nature
Michigan	Mich Comp Laws §750.158	Crime against nature
	Mich Comp Laws §750.338	Gross indecency; female persons
Missouri	Mo. Rev. Stat. §566.090	Sexual misconduct
Montana	Mont. Code §45-5-505	Deviate sexual conduct
Nevada	Nev. Rev. Stat. §201.190	Crime against nature
New Jersey	N.J. Rev. Stat. §2c:14-4	Lewdness [public]
Oklahoma	Okla. Stat. tit.21 §886	Crime against nature
S. Carolina	S. C. Code §16-15-120	Buggery
Texas	Tex. Crim. Code §2106	Homosexual Conduct
Utah	Utah Code §76-5-403	Sodomy—forcible sodomy
Vermont	Vt. Stat. tit.13 §2601	Lewd and lascivious conduct [public]
Virginia	Va. Code §18.2-361	Crime against nature

ENDNOTES

1. See Rose v. Locke, 423 U.S. 48 (1975).

2. People v. Livermore, 9 Mich. App. 47, , 155 N.W. 2d 711, 712 (Mich. Ct. App. 1968).

3. For example, the District of Columbia statute entitled Sodomy provides in part that in any indictment for such offenses "it shall not be necessary to set forth the particular unnatural or perverted sexual practice with the commission of

which the defendant may be charged, nor to set forth the particular manner in which said unnatural or perverted sexual practice was committed."

4. As one judge states, "the sordid unnatural acts testified to by this witness are such that little could be gained by setting them forth in this opinion." Warner v. State, 189 P.2d 526 (Cr. Ct. App. Okl. 1971) (case involved "oral sodomy" between two women and between a woman and a man).

5. All italicized passages are excerpted and slightly edited from JUDITH MC-DANIEL, JUST SAY YES (Ithaca, New York: Firebrand Books 1990). The passages appear on pages 15, 36, 124-5, 67-8, and 172.

6. *Buggery* is often used interchangeably with *sodomy,* but according to BLACK'S LAW DICTIONARY, even when so used it does not necessarily include fellatio. There are no reported cases interpreting the South Carolina statute.

7. Thompson v. Aldredge, 200 S.E. 799 (1939).

8. State v. Young, 193 So. 2d 243 (La. 1967).

9. Warner v. State, 489 P.2d 526 (Cr. Ct. App. Okl. 1971).

10. Saylers v. State, 755 P.2d 97 (Cr. Ct. App. Okl. 1988).

PRIVACY

4

SEXUAL PRIVACY

Challenges to the lesbian sex statutes are necessary, but they can also be domesticating. Court challenges have generally focused on the question of privacy, but such a notion can itself be domesticating, especially in the context of lesbian sexual expression. There is nothing inherently private about sex. Legal notions of sexual privacy are rooted in the (heterosexual) couple. Two people engaged in sexual intimacy enjoy the privileges of privacy, but the addition of a third partner means that the same sorts of sexual intimacies are not private. Sexual privacy also requires the sexually private couple to be in a private place. Privacy can be purchased, and it is ultimately dependent on the legally sacred concept of private property. While we sometimes think of sexual privacy as at odds with the rule of law, it is integral and especially useful in allowing the rule of law to be the rule of men over women.

All of the above notwithstanding, sexual privacy can be a wedge used in the service of lesbian survival. Given the available legal concepts, sexual privacy is a possible argument to guarantee at least certain rights to lesbians. Although based on constitutional values usually derived from due process, the words *privacy* and *sexual* do not appear in the United States Constitution. A handful of states, such as Montana and Florida (both of which continue to criminalize lesbian sex) have amended their state constitutions to provide for an unspecified right to privacy. Apart from these exceptional state constitutions, the absence of a constitutional grounding for privacy causes problems. Privacy is the doctrinal base for the eroding constitutional right to abortion and the unsuccessful federal attacks on state laws criminalizing lesbian and gay sex. Conservative forces effectively argue the "illegitimacy" of sexual privacy based on its absence from the language of the federal constitution. In the face of such attacks, we often defend and celebrate privacy.

We need to be more critical of privacy, however, not only because its vitality as a legal strategy is subject to criticism, but because its legal power threatens to domesticate both lesbian sex and lesbian lives. When we think of our sexuality in terms of the legal concept of privacy, we become confused. We want to be both private and public. We want to be able to say that our sexuality is no one's business, and we want to be out of every closet. We can be convinced that such desires are contradictory if we accept what is often called the public/private split enforced by the rule of law.

Our confusion reflects a confusion in the history of privacy itself. Privacy as a positive political concept is rooted in liberal individualism's glorification of the autonomous person, at least as long as he is male, white, over twenty-one, and has a suitable expanse of (private) property. Originally, however, privacy was a negative concept: a lack. Derived from a Latin term that means to be "without public office," it is related to words like *deprivation* and *bereavement*. This tension between privacy as individual freedom and privacy as an absence of community persists.

Within contemporary lesbianism, this tension exhibits itself in our everyday discussions and is exemplified by the so-called S/M debates which continue to provoke controversy. The cross-accusations within these debates are enlightening. Many of the pro-S/M (also called pro-sex) lesbians accuse those who disagree with them of being more feminist than lesbian, while the anti-S/M lesbians accuse those who disagree with them of being more gay (male) than lesbian. These cross-accusations refer not only to cultural and political concerns, but to specific legal controversies revolving around issues of sexual privacy. Most notable is the gay (and lesbian) legal activist constitutional challenge to sex statutes, and the feminist advancement and arguments against pornography laws. Both of these legal controversies influence—and domesticate—the ways in which we think about lesbian sexual privacy in nonlegal contexts.

Gay Rights and Sexual Privacy

Gay, lesbian, and bisexual legal activists have long been engaged in attempts to eliminate the statutes that criminalize our sexual behaviors, some of which were discussed in the last chapter. Mounting a constitutional challenge required that someone have a sufficient stake in the action to satisfy the legal requirement of standing. Because the statutes were rarely enforced, or enforced only in public or nonconsensual or nonadult situations, the statutes were insulated from constitutional challenge. Numerous courts dismissed actions challenging the sex laws for a failure to satisfy standing requirements.

In Atlanta in August of 1982, activists located the nearly perfect case with which to present the claim that the Georgia statute criminalizing oral/anal sex violated constitutional notions of privacy. An Atlanta police officer with a grudge against Michael Hardwick arrested Hardwick in his own bedroom for committing the crime of sodomy with a consenting adult male. Michael Hardwick was charged and "bound over to the Superior Court." Although the District Attorney decided not to prosecute the case "unless further evidence developed," the arrest and court appearance were sufficient to confer standing on Michael Hardwick. Hardwick became a plaintiff in a civil rights suit, joined by a married heterosexual couple, challenging the Georgia statute. Although the statute makes no reference to gender or marriage, the married couple's claims that they were unconstitutionally chilled from engaging in the sex prohibited by the statute were not enough to overcome their lack of evidence showing a likelihood of prosecution, and the court dismissed them for not satisfying the standing requirement.

Hardwick lost his claim in the federal trial court but won at the next appellate level, the United States Court of Appeals for the Eleventh Circuit, encompassing much of the deep South. Judge Johnson, a well-known civil rights champion from Montgomery, Alabama, wrote an opinion in which he found that the Georgia statute implicated the "fundamental right" to an activity that is "quintessentially private."[1] The United States Supreme Court—the ultimate arbiter of constitutional doctrine—agreed to review the case, a relatively rare occurrence given the percentage of requests for review filed with the Court. Although there were leaks that the Court was ready to rule in favor of Hardwick, and one Justice said, after retiring, that he had made a mistake by not taking a pro-Hardwick position, the United States Supreme Court ruled against Hardwick. The opinion issued in 1986, and still the law of the land, states that any claim that homosexual sodomy is protected by constitutional privacy is "facetious, at best."[2]

The critiques of the Hardwick opinion in the legal community —and there are many—are essentially critiques of the Court's failure to honor the principles of liberal individualism that support privacy doctrine. Typical critiques have titles like "A Man's Home is No Longer His Castle." Such titles illustrate the gendered character of privacy doctrine. The *Hardwick* opinion itself, and an overwhelming amount of the commentary about the opinion, either fail to mention lesbianism or mention it only in the same breath as "heterosexual sodomy," as if both lesbianism and heterosexuality were marginal to the real issue of gay male sexuality.

This is not to say that the *Hardwick* litigation was solely based on liberal individual privacy reasoning, or that it was entirely a gay male affair. There are many strains of community values and coalition work, as well as lesbian labor, influence, and politics. One of the main evidences of both community and lesbianism is the amicus curiae (friend of the court) brief filed by San Francisco attorney Mary Dunlap on behalf of the National Lesbian Rights Project. This brief makes specific analogies to historical cases limiting the rights of women, of African-Americans, and of Japanese-Americans, all since overturned by the Court.[3] Nevertheless, the main argument advanced by constitutional law scholar and Harvard Professor Laurence Tribe, arguing for Hardwick, and the argument adopted by dissenting Justice Blackmun's opinion, as well as the position advanced in most of the critiques of the majority's opinion, are all sophisticated versions of "a man's home is his castle."

One of the major cases supporting this view of privacy is *Stanley v. Georgia*,[4] a case relied upon quite heavily by the advocates for *Hardwick*. In *Stanley*, the United States Supreme Court held that the right to privacy protected the viewing of pornography within the confines of one's home. While there are some legal questions about the viability of *Stanley* as precedent for *Hardwick*, almost everyone agreed that Mr. Stanley's expression of his sexuality by viewing pornography in his own home was analogous to Michael Hardwick's expression of his sexuality by engaging in sex with another man in his own home. This comparison highlights the grounding of privacy in liberal individualism: there must be an individual (man) and he must have (private) property. The only boundary to a king's privacy rights within his castle is the so-called harm principle: his actions must not harm anyone else. The need to satisfy the harm principle explains the emphasis on pornography as a victimless crime in *Stanley* and on the consent of Michael Hardwick's partner in *Hardwick*. However, although relied upon by the amicus brief in favor of Michael Hardwick filed by the National Organization for Women, *Stanley*'s assumption that pornography is victimless presents problems for many feminists.

Feminism and Sexual Privacy

For feminists, that a man's home is his castle can be the bedrock of marital domestic violence. Men's privacy has been the rationale supporting legal rules such as the rule of thumb (a husband can beat his wife with a stick unless the stick is thicker than his thumb) and the marital rape exemption (a man cannot legally rape his wife). Yet feminism has often sought to simply replace *man* with *woman*. As a legal reform movement, feminism has capitalized on woman's privacy, especially in the concept of decisional privacy which supports a woman's right to choose an abortion, other birth control, or other reproductive techniques. Yet even in the area of reproduction, the concepts of privacy and choice betray their roots in liberal individualism's commitment to property when contractual arrangements such as surrogate mothering are upheld by invoking a woman's rights to privacy and free choice, or when the right to abortion is restricted to women who can purchase it.

The most ardent indictment of the possibility of privacy as a doctrine with any meaning for women comes from feminist legal theorist Catherine MacKinnon. MacKinnon states: "No law takes away women's privacy. Most women do not have any to take, and no law gives them what they do not already have."[5] MacKinnon explicitly rejects liberal individualism (as well as Marxism), and her theories often share disturbing similarities with conservative majoritarian forces, despite MacKinnon's ultimate goal of emancipation. The charge of conservativism was most heatedly debated and litigated in the context of MacKinnon's pornography ordinance.

The pornography ordinance that MacKinnon drafted with Andrea Dworkin is often called the Minneapolis ordinance, although it did not become law in that city. The ordinance did become law in Indianapolis, and it was in its Indianapolis incarnation that it reached both a federal trial and federal appellate court. Both courts found that the ordinance violated the first amendment's guarantee of free speech, and the United States Supreme Court entered a one-line affirmance.[6]

The ordinance's purpose is to empower women by allowing them to file civil actions in cases of pornography, defined as the "graphic explicit subordination of women, whether in pictures or words," that includes various scenarios such as women enjoying pain or humiliation, women as servile and—interesting to consider in the context of the last chapter—as "being penetrated by objects or animals." Yet other feminists argued in the courts, in an amicus curiae brief known as the FACT (Feminist Anti-Censorship Taskforce) brief, that the ordinance actually is "particularly detrimental to women" and "discriminates on the basis of sex and reinforces sexist stereotypes."[7] The FACT brief relies quite strongly on notions of privacy, and situates sexual choices within the realm of liberal individualism. While this is not the only time that feminist legal reformers have disagreed about legal strategies, the depth of the disagreement about this ordinance is profound.

The feminist legal controversy surrounding the pornography ordinance, like the *Hardwick* litigation, involves lesbian labor, influence, and politics. One result of this lesbianism is an acknowledgment of the very different views women can have of male domination and sexual expression. In stereotypical terms, this difference is the one between a wife abused by a husband who uses pornography to give him ideas for further sexual violence in support of male domination, and a lesbian respectfully loving another woman who uses pornography to provide information for further sexual exploration of the sexuality historically denied her. Clearly our private lives influence our views on sexual privacy.

The pornography controversy is not simply about differing personal lives, however, but also about the role of the rule of law in our lives. As such, it is similar to one of the central questions that marks *Lesbian (Out)law:* when can we use the law and when are we being used by it? In the area of sexual privacy, our answers are complicated not only by our difficult relationship to the rule of law, but also by our history with sexual privacy. The Roman laws that allowed a man to privately execute a woman suspected of lesbian sexual expression discussed in chapter 2 are but one example of the fact that the privatization of our sexuality does not necessarily guarantee safety.

If privatization does not mean safety, neither does a public rule of law. The most horrifying specter raised by the pornography ordinance—again using a stereotypical example—is that of Phyllis Shafly (any woman qualifies under the ordinance) bringing a civil action against JoAnn Loulan for her books and workshops on lesbian sexuality on the grounds that all lesbianism is degrading and that Loulan discusses penetration by objects. Imagine a judge (statistically a white middle-class heterosexual man) listening to expert testimony about lesbian sexual practices and then ruling whether such practices were degrading. Imagine this scenario in a state with one of the lesbian sex statutes discussed in the previous chapter. It is this imagined specter that led lesbians thinking about the pornography ordinance to frequently quote Audre Lorde—"the master's tools will never dismantle the master's house,"[8]—despite the fact that the same lesbians were using the master's legal tools in the *Hardwick* litigation and in lawsuits arguing for positive protections in the law for lesbians.

Sexual privacy has not been a successful doctrinal master's tool for lesbians. In *Hardwick*, it was not sufficient to override the lesbian sex statutes that criminalize our sexual practices as perverted, unnatural, and deviant. In the pornography ordinance litigation, lesbians argued on both sides of the issue. However, because many lesbians, especially well-known lesbians working with independent lesbian and feminist publishers, were signatories to the FACT brief (which itself mentions *lesbianism* only twice and *sexual minorities* once), we often identify lesbians as prevailing. Yet any success is not attributable to the vitality of our sexual privacy under the rule of law. The triumph belongs to the plaintiffs in the case, the American Booksellers Association (ABA), a multimillion dollar publishing business organization. This organization had no need to argue sexual privacy. It could ground its legal arguments in the First Amendment's free speech clause because the ordinance directly regulated writings and pictures. The ABA had no problem meeting the legal requirement of standing because it alleged the possibility of economic injury. Although having among its membership many of the independent lesbian, feminist, and gay presses, the ABA is an organization ultimately supported by Random House and *Penthouse,* themselves an integral part of corporate conglomerate America. Sexual privacy, to the extent it is recognized, must exist as an appendage to private property, preferably lots of it.

Lesbianism and Sexual Privacy

In the controversies over sexual privacy pervasive in our communities—issues like lesbian S/M and lesbians sleeping with men—we seem to center lesbians and put law at the margins. Our discussions occur in the pages of our publications, at our festivals, and on our living room (and bedroom) floors, rather than in briefs, in court, or around legal conference room tables. There is little overt reference to the rule of law, and when there is, everyone seems to agree that the law is extraneous. I don't think I have ever heard a lesbian propose that we draft a statute or ordinance making lesbian S/M, for example, a crime.

Surprisingly, then, legalism permeates our discourse. We throw around labels like *lesbian sex police* and *sexual outlaws.* We use notions of sexual privacy to argue that any sexual acts within the privacy of someone's home are her business and no other lesbian's, and we use those same notions to argue that the wearing of sexual symbols (such as S/M gear) should not be displayed in public because they invade other lesbians' privacy. Like the *Hardwick* and pornography litigations, we ground our judgments in freedom of speech or in the impossibility of "victimlessness," in liberal individualism or in emancipatory values. We enforce our judgments with ostracism, a punishment akin to banishment and based upon the same theories as imprisonment. Without explicitly appealing to the rule of law, we appeal to the concepts—and violence—embodied in the rule of law.

Our appeal has a certain poignancy when we consider *Hardwick* and the economic status of our lesbian presses compared with mainstream publishing giants, but I am more concerned with the domestication of our discourse that our appeal to legalism produces. While there are many explanations for our vigorous debates about sexual privacy, it seems to me that our controversies are about the boundaries of lesbianism. If lesbians define ourselves (at least in part) by our sexuality, then the boundaries of this sexuality are integral to our identity. I do not agree, therefore, with conclusions that arguments about our sexuality are deflective or counterproductive. We need to argue and consider our sexualities.

Our discourse must belong to us, though, and not be defined by the terms set by the dominant legal culture. Sexual privacy is unpredictable terrain for lesbians: it works neither as a failsafe guarantee nor as a consistent obstacle. When we appropriate its terms into our own concerns unthinkingly, because those are the concepts that inhere in our common sense, we appropriate all the inconsistencies. Our thinking becomes confused and dualistic. We also remain domesticated by the rule of law. The concepts of sexual privacy are rooted in the rule of men over women and over property. Our sexuality has different roots.

REFERENCES

Ruthann Robson, *Lifting Belly: Privacy, Sexuality and Lesbianism,* 12 WOMEN'S RIGHTS LAW REPORTER 177 (1990).

ENDNOTES

1. Hardwick v. Bowers, 760 F.2d 1202 (11th Cir. 1985).

2. Bowers v. Hardwick, 478 U.S. 186 (1986).

3. This brief is reprinted at 14 N.Y.U. REVIEW OF LAW AND SOCIAL CHANGE 949 (1986).

4. 394 U.S. 557 (1969).

5. CATHERINE MACKINNON, TOWARD A FEMINIST THEORY OF THE STATE 239 (1989).

6. American Bookseller's Ass'n v. Hudnut, 598 F.Supp. 1316 (S.D. In. 1984), affirmed 771 F.2d 323 (7th Cir. 1985), affirmed by memorandum opinion, 475 U.S. 1001 (1986).

7. The FACT brief is reprinted at 21 JOURNAL OF LAW REFORM 76 (1987-88).

8. AUDRE LORDE, SISTER OUTSIDER 112 (Freedom, California: Crossing Press 1984).

5

PUBLIC EXPOSURE

The legal concept of privacy is relevant not only as a shield to prevent the intrusions of prosecution, or persecution of our sexual acts, but also as a buffer against the public exposure of our sexual identities. We can sue for the tort of invasion of privacy if someone has revealed private facts and caused harm to our peace of mind. For lesbians, this tort (a civil action in which money is awarded) implicates our control of information about our sexuality: how and when we are out.

Yet judicial interpretations of the tort serve the rule of law rather than lesbians. A case involving a gay man is relevant. Oliver (Bill) Sipple sued various newspapers for revealing his homosexuality. Sipple garnered some limelight when he grabbed Sara Jane Moore's arm as she was attempting to assassinate President Ford in 1975. A San Francisco columnist reported on Sipple's heroism, and added that Sipple frequented a well-known gay bar and was a close friend of "Gay Politico" Harvey Milk. The *L.A. Times* speculated that the absence of a thank-you telegram from the White House for saving the president's life could be attributed to the fact that the "husky ex-marine hero" Bill Sipple was gay. Similar stories were picked up by out-of-state papers. The trial and appellate courts both rejected Sipple's claim for invasion of privacy, ruling that his sexuality was not private and could not therefore be invaded. The fact that "his parents, brothers and sisters learned for the first time of his homosexual orientation" in the newspaper reports and "abandoned" him as a result was irrelevant compared to his activities within the gay community. The California court also thought Sipple's sexuality was newsworthy (and thus not protected) because the stories were prompted by "legitimate political considerations, i.e., to dispel the false public notion that gays were timid, weak, and unheroic figures and to raise the equally important question whether the President of the United States entertained a discriminatory attitude or bias against a minority group such as homosexuals."[1]

Sipple's choice not to come out to his family is legally overridden by his activity within his community and his exceptionality to discriminatory stereotypes. Both of these rationales are disturbing. There is no recognition that our communities are in any way unique: the Castro is like suburban Cincinnati, the *Male Express* like the *L.A. Times*. From the standpoint of the rule of law, our communities are simply assimilable. The dominant culture is the only culture; biases of the dominant culture control. Any nonconformance to those biases is noteworthy, newsworthy, and part of the public domain. These rationales would limit privacy only to the most closeted and stereotypical lesbian. Whatever one thinks of Sipple's decision to sue, or his impulse to save then-President Ford's life, our general notions of privacy would seem to give him certain guarantees in the realm of revealing his sexual orientation to his biological family. Privacy under the rule of law includes no such rule.

The tort of invasion of privacy implicitly admits the truth of the fact revealed. When the fact is false, one sues for defamation, also known as libel or slander. Truth, as a defense to a defamation action, can place the meanings of our sexual identities on trial. The nineteenth-century Woods/Pirie case discussed previously did this, as the British judges ruminated on whether the allegations of lesbianism were true considering the facts, class backgrounds, religious influences, and their constructions of lesbianism. A contemporary case might revolve around definitional boundaries. For example, imagine a trial brought by a celebrity against a tabloid, newspaper, or action group on the basis of this statement: "She's absolutely queer." If the truth of the statement were raised as a defense, the jury would have to decide upon the meaning of "absolutely," not to mention "queer." What if the evidence included three men testifying that they had sexual relations with the celebrity? What if twenty women testified that they had sexual relations with her? Under the rule of law, a statement like "absolutely queer" can either be only true or false. The verdict must either be for the plaintiff celebrity or the defendant responsible for the statement's publication. It might be possible that the entire case would depend upon the interpretation of "absolutely," although I suspect it would actually depend upon the jury members' ideas about sexuality.

The celebrity is entitled to money if she wins so that she will be compensated for the damage to her reputation. Generally, she would have to prove a specific harm or damage, such as the withdrawal of an offer of a starring role in a film. When a defamatory statement is especially deplorable, however, the law will generously assume damage to one's reputation. Many courts have held that allegations of lesbianism or male homosexuality fit into the category *deplorable*. Some courts support this with general notions of morality, or prejudice, or specifically with a criminal sex statute.[2] Calling someone a lesbian is like calling her a burglar or a murderer.

Legal concepts of privacy and public exposure, as well as the specter of defamation, pervade our current discussions of outing, the practice of publicizing a mainstream celebrity's gay or lesbian identity. The outing controversy has captured the attention of the mainstream media—to a degree that the lesbian S/M debates never came close to approaching—and newspapers and magazines regularly report on outing, often providing tantalizing details and clues without subjecting themselves to lawsuits by actually naming names. Like the S/M debates, we again discuss the controversy in legal terms. There are amazingly diverse people who use the First Amendment's freedom of speech clause to support often opposing positions. I often hear the terms *libel* and *slander* bandied about; I read about invasions of privacy; I listen to pronouncements about public-figure status.

The outing controversy captures important issues for lesbians, such as passing, heterosexism, and the boundaries of lesbian identity. Yet it is often presented and discussed as if it is a legal (or legal-moral) issue. Law's enshrinement of privacy takes the center stage, and lesbian survival is marginalized.

This marginalization is highlighted when the law enforces rather than protects privacy. Enforced privatization—censorship—occurs under the rule of law's exceptions to the First Amendment's guarantee of freedom of speech. The First Amendment itself can be used to preclude chosen self-exposure. Using the First Amendment, courts have upheld the decisions of college newspapers not to include ads for lesbian roommates or a gay counseling center, and the phone company's decision to cancel a yellow pages ad for a gay and lesbian bookstore. Interestingly in these litigations, one issue is whether the University of Nebraska school newspaper, the Mississippi State University school newspaper, and the monopoly called Bell Telephone are public entities that might be held to a higher standard of fairness than mere private individuals. The courts have no trouble concluding that these student newspapers at public universities and the telephone company are really private.[3]

Under the rules of law categorizing what is public and what is private, Bill Sipple's sexuality is public. Ma Bell's yellow pages are private. This absurdity can be explained by the intricacies within the rules of law. The ultimate explanation, however, is privacy's dependence upon private property. Control of the means to disseminate information allows one a measure of self-determination about one's privacy. Although there is still the possibility of government censorship, the slogan of the lesbian and feminist print movement that "freedom belongs to she who owns the presses" has continued vitality.

The threat of deprivation of property enforces privacy, even when privacy is unwanted. As the next chapter discusses, there is little legal protection against economic discrimination for those who reveal their lesbianism. The First Amendment does not protect a school employee fired because she discussed her bisexuality and lesbianism with her coworkers. The courts conclude that "her personal sexual orientation is not a matter of public concern."[4] Unlike Bill Sipple, whose "personal sexual orientation" is judicially declared to be a matter of public concern, her sexual orientation is privatized beyond the protection of the First Amendment. This privatization to her detriment continues even if the school board members convey the private fact of her sexuality to another prospective employer. According to a recent case, this communication would be insulated by the legal doctrine of privileged—private—communication.[5] If she does not obtain employment in the school system because she is a lesbian, this is merely a private problem.

Notions of public and private can be routinely used to deny a lesbian the relief she seeks. A lesbian's sexuality is too public, and thus her privacy cannot be invaded because she does not have any. Or a lesbian's sexuality is merely private, and thus her discussions of it do not rise to the level of protectable public concern. Legal theories of the public and private are not theories that guarantee the survival of lesbians.

The tension between the private and the public is a tension maintained by the rule of law. When we put lesbians at the center, it is not that this tension disappears; rather, it no longer makes sense.

Our sexuality does not belong to the public sphere or the private one. It belongs only to us.

ENDNOTES

1. Sipple v. Chronicle Publishing Company, 154 Cal. App. 3d 1040, 201 Cal. Rptr. 665 (1984).

2. See Head v. Newton, 596 S.W.2d 209 (Civ. Ct. App. Texas 1980); Mazart v. State, 109 Misc. 2d 1092, 441 N.Y.S.2d 600 (1981). Compare Dally v. Orange County, 117 A.D.2d 577, 497 N.Y.S.2d 947 (1986) (after New York's sex statute declared unconstitutional, court nevertheless found statement of homosexuality defamatory without need for proof of damages because "rightly or wrongly, many individuals still view homosexuality as immoral").

In an unreported case in which the court found that "fag" and "faggot" said in the context of a "bar room fight" were not sufficiently derogatory, the court relied upon the absence of any criminal statute as well as upon Wisconsin's sexual orientation antidiscrimination laws. Lehman v. Wellens, 407 N.W.2d 567 (1987) (unpublished opinion, text in WESTLAW).

3. Sinn v. Daily Nebraskan, 829 F.2d 662 (8th Cir. 1987); Mississippi Gay Alliance v. Goudelock, 536 F.2d 1073 (5th Cir. 1976); Loring v. BellSouth Advertising and Publishing Co., 177 Ga. App. 307, 339 S.E.2d 372 (1985).

4. Rowland v. Mad River School District, 730 F.2d 444 (6th Cir. 1984), cert. denied 470 U.S. 1009 (1985).

5. See Boehm v. American Bankers Insurance Group, Inc., 557 So. 2d 91 (3rd DCA Fla. 1990) (statements by company president that former employee was a homosexual made in "private conference" to executive search agent were not actionable defamation or tortious interference with business relationship).

THE REGULATION OF LESBIANISM

6

DISCOURSES OF DISCRIMINATION

For those who believe that equality is an elemental rule of law, the discourse of discrimination is a disappointment. The Constitution includes a clause guaranteeing "equal protection of the laws," but this equal protection does not extend to lesbians as lesbians. There is nothing in current constitutional doctrine that prevents those otherwise bound by the Constitution (public or state-type entities) from discriminating on the basis of lesbianism. Thus, a school board can refuse to hire you in accordance with a policy that declares lesbians unsuitable employees; a manager can refuse to rent to you because he wants to maintain a "family atmosphere" in the project; a coach can exclude you from a basketball team because she thinks lesbians present an undesirable image for women's sports; and a library can refuse to issue you a library card because statistics show lesbians are chronic late-returners of borrowed books.

A lesbian using constitutional doctrine to protest discrimination will be more successful if she uses another facet of her identity. She can argue that she is being discriminated against on the basis of her race, religion, or nationality. While the power of such arguments has certainly been eroded within the last decade, they remain the most highly recognized claims entitled to consideration, if not vindication.

The recognition of claims based on race, religion, or nationality is predicated on the legal concept of the suspect class. Race is the paradigm suspect class because of the historical development of the equality doctrine. Despite the "all men are created equal" words of the Declaration of Independence, notions of equality did not appear in the United States Constitution until Reconstruction, the postslavery period following the Civil War. Even after being added to the Constitution, equality has not been consistently interpreted. With regard to race, integration is a relatively recent phenomenon; separate-but-equal was the prevailing standard for many years. Contemporary discrimination discourse judges racial classifications as suspect classifications, and as such they are subjected to the strictest scrutiny. Only the most compelling interest will be able to override racial classifications, and courts usually declare such classifications unconstitutional.

The hallmarks of a suspect class are thus derived from legal notions of race. Traditionally, a suspect class must be a social minority that has been historically discriminated against and continues to be relatively politically powerless, and its members must possess immutable characteristics that are identifiable. Although these criteria are certainly not absolute, arguments that lesbians are within a suspect class based on sexual orientation must work within the traditional hallmarks.[1] The most troublesome factor is the immutable identifiable characteristic. Discussions of the applicability of this factor lead to debates whether lesbianism is an identity or an activity. For legal protection, it must be an identity, and a relatively unchanging one.

The courts have not found sexual orientation to be the basis for a suspect class. Although there are exceptions (usually in cases that have been reversed), the prevailing judicial discourse is that lesbianism is an activity not an identity. As an activity, it can be criminalized; as a nonidentity it is not entitled to equality. Courts have little difficulty manipulating the criteria so that even discriminatory regulations or statements that refer to sexual orientation as an identity are reinterpreted to mean sexual activity. For example, a court has concluded that a statement that one is a lesbian "can rationally and reasonably be viewed as reliable evidence of a desire and propensity to engage in homosexual acts," and is "compelling evidence" that one "has in the past and is likely again to engage in such conduct." That the conduct is criminalized supports discrimination, not—according to the court—on the basis "merely upon her status as a lesbian, but upon reasonable inferences about her probable conduct in the past and in the future."[2] While the statement "I am a lesbian" is tantamount to "I am someone who engages in (criminal) activity," it is insufficient to invoke the protections of suspect class identity. Further, because the activity is or can be criminalized, the rule of law refuses to recognize it as a fundamental right. The failure to do so for equal protection purposes is linked to the failure to extend due process/privacy protections to lesbianism, as discussed in chapter 4. The rule of law often seems like a self-sustaining maze.

Most attorneys, myself included, have learned to maneuver sufficiently in the rule of law's labyrinth to construct an argument that lesbianism fits into one of the law's favored categories, such as suspect class. This argument rests on lesbian as an identity that is relatively immutable, a minority that has been historically discriminated against as well as being politically powerless. I think there is nothing wrong with making such legal arguments. As a strategy for gaining a measure of protection, equality doctrine holds some promise, although it is generally unfulfilled.

The problem is that the legal necessity for arguing immutable identity can infiltrate our own conceptualizing about ourselves. Just as sociological notions of stigma and social constructionism, and psychological notions of archetypes and inversions, can dominate our own theorizing, legal standards can dominate and domesticate. Arguments in legal journals that advocate on behalf of lesbian and gay issues often include a section about sexual orientation being determined early in one's life and thus not within one's control. This strategy is akin to throwing ourselves on the mercy of the court because we cannot help ourselves for our sexuality. I find such a strategy not only domesticating, but humiliating. Whether or not we believe any of the causes articulated for lesbian identity formation, our beliefs should be independent of the influence of the rule of law.

The development of the so-called ethnic model of sexual orientation—lesbians, gay males, and bisexuals as members of a culture similar to an ethnic/racial one—is a partial reflection of legal dominance. The law's dichotomies between identity and activity, minority and majority, powerlessness and empowerment, reenforce dichotomies from other disciplines, such as the dichotomy between lesbian as a noun or verb, as essential or socially constructed, as innate or chosen. Yet such dichotomies may not reflect our experiences. We talk about who we are and what we do in the same breath. Ask a hundred different lesbians about identities and acts, and there will be a thousand different answers. We are not reducible to any identity captured by the category *lesbian*, nor are we reducible to our sexual activities.

The paradigm of the suspect class developed in the context of legal responses to race has little intrinsic meaning for lesbian theorizing about ourselves. In fact, recent radical race theory likewise suggests that it has little intrinsic meaning for racial theorizing.[3] Choices to use such legal principles can be valid ones, but we must remember that they are concepts developed by men, under the rule of law, intended to extend the rules to other men.

A lesbian can also argue discrimination on the basis of gender. Legally, gender is not entitled to the strict scrutiny of racial classifications; it is only quasi-suspect. Courts applying a constitutional analysis to a discriminatory act subject gender classifications to "intermediate scrutiny" and engage in a balancing test. Gender classifications are nevertheless more often declared invalid than sexual orientation classifications. Because sexual orientation is not a suspect class, it is subject to only minimal scrutiny under constitutional equality doctrine. Any rational basis will be sufficient to uphold a sexual orientation classification. In a circular fashion, courts sustain rationales derived from the public governmental entity's right to make discriminatory decisions: a school board's interest in education is a sufficient rationale for excluding lesbian teachers; the CIA's interest in national security is similarly sufficient, as is the military's interest in national defense as discussed in the next chapter.

Federal constitutional notions of equality prohibit discriminatory gender classifications, as well as race, nationality, and religion classifications, by public entities. Title VII, a portion of the federal 1964 Civil Rights Act, prohibits similar types of discrimination by private employers, at least if they employ over fifteen persons. While employment discrimination has the highest profile, federal statutes also prohibit discrimination in housing, education, accommodations, and government contracts. Gender, or as it says in Title VII, "sex," was added to the bill not because of forward-looking feminists, but because a conservative congressman thought it was an amusing addition that would insure the bill's defeat. Sexual orientation was apparently not funny enough for inclusion and has not yet been taken seriously enough to merit incorporation. Proposals to amend the statute to include "affectional or sexual orientation" have, in fact, been introduced in both the Senate and House of Representatives several times in recent years, and many lesbian and gay legal reformers believe the amendment will eventually be adopted.

Feminist legal reformers and theorists, however, have recently been arguing that the sex classification in both federal constitutional doctrine and Title VII be interpreted to encompass sexual orientation. This has not always been the case. When the feminist legal reform movement had the Equal Rights Amendment (ERA) foremost on its agenda, many of its adherents argued that sex discrimination meant only discrimination on the basis of biological sex; it did not include discrimination on the basis of lesbianism. Although the federal ERA failed, the argument that *sex* means *gender* to the exclusion of sexual preference prevailed. Courts construing federal constitutional equality doctrine, Title VII, as well as state-adopted ERAs, have uniformly ruled this way. First the judicial discourse creates a category *homosexual*. Then it concludes that within that category, male and female homosexuals are equal. If one argued in a discrimination case that lesbians were being discriminated against as compared with gay men, a valid claim for sex discrimination might exist.[4] Obviously, this is unacceptable.

Yet the current legal feminist reform position collapsing lesbianism and sexual orientation and gender is also unacceptable from a lesbian-centered view. The legal feminist reform movement, so conscientious about perceiving the gendering of other categories, lapses into its own ungendered category—sexual orientation. That lesbians, gay men, and bisexual women and men might have legally distinct concerns is unimagined. Heterosexuality is the paradigm, and all deviations from it constitute a single category. Further, sexual orientation, even ungendered, is not gender. While gender and sexual orientation are certainly intertwined, they are not coextensive. One would not argue, for example, that a provision against discrimination on the basis of sexual orientation includes gender. The opposite argument, that sex discrimination includes sexual orientation, subordinates lesbianism to feminism. Such a subordination does have strategic advantages since sex discrimination is a recognized legal wrong while sexual orientation discrimination generally is not. However, it is ultimately unacceptable. It was unacceptable as a strategy to attempt to secure passage of the ERA by excluding lesbians, and it is unacceptable as a strategy to expand the reach of gender discrimination by including lesbians.

In addition to gender discrimination law, there are other laws that might encompass prohibitions against discrimination on the basis of lesbianism. These preexisting laws have been used to support creative litigative strategies. Civil services rules, tenure rules, union rules, and other rules that include a "good cause" requirement can be used as the foundation for an argument that a lesbian cannot be fired on the basis of her lesbianism.

One example is the first in a series of cases involving a gay Eagle Scout who was denied the routinely granted status of scoutmaster by the Mount Diablo Council of the Boy Scouts of America on the basis of his homosexuality. He sued, and a trial court dismissed his claims. He appealed to a California appellate court which held that he had a right to present his claims further. The appellate court concluded that expulsion of the gay boy scout could violate a common law (i.e., nonstatutory) right of fair procedure unless the Boy Scouts could prove a connection between the Scout's homosexuality and "any danger of harm to the association." The court also ruled that the expulsion could violate California's Unruh Act prohibiting discrimination. In considering the Unruh Act, the court reasoned that the act's particular references to classifications such as sex and race were meant to be illustrative and not restrictive. Thus, the court did not subordinate sexuality to gender, but read the statute broadly as mandating equality.[5]

The California appellate court's reasoning in the Boy Scout case demonstrates how specific rules of law can be liberally interpreted to render discrimination on the basis of sexual orientation unlawful. The emphasis is on interpretation. This panel of judges, given another set of submissions from the attorneys, could have reached the same conclusion but based it on entirely different legal rules, including the constitutional equality principles and federal antidiscrimination statute discussed above. And given the same common law and antidiscrimination act, another panel of judges in another part of California or in another year could have easily reached an opposite conclusion and written an equally persuasive opinion. In fact, when the case finally came to trial in 1991, this is exactly what happened. The trial judge ruled that the the Boy Scouts' policy of excluding gays did not violate the California Unruh Act's prohibition against discrimination. The case is being appealed.

The immense discretion possessed by those with the power to interpret the rules of law is usually exercised against protective possibilities for people like gay Boy Scouts and lesbian Girl Scouts. Thus, lesbian and gay rights legal reformers have been seeking rules of law that would narrow discretion in the direction of providing more protective possibilities for lesbians and gay men. Given the failure of efforts under federal constitutional doctrine and Title VII, reformers have focused on state and local levels. In 1991, there were four states with statutes making discrimination on the basis of sexual orientation unlawful: Wisconsin (since 1982), Massachusetts (since 1989), Hawaii and Connecticut (both in 1991). Many states have witnessed intensive efforts to pass these statutes, and numerous failures often preceded the successes. These few victories hold out the promise that defeats in other states are only temporary.

At the local level, close to 100 towns, cities, and counties now have laws that prohibit discrimination on the basis of sexual orientation. While a few ordinances have been in effect since the mid-1970s, such as the one in Berkeley, most are much more recent. The passing of these ordinances has been the focus of intense energies. In many instances, there have been referenda, recalls, repeals, and registration drives. Such grassroots organizing surfaces the differences in our approaches both to lesbianism and to law. Do we demand equality based on our differences, or based on our sameness except for the small detail of the gender of our sexual partner? Do we compare sexual orientation to ethnic and racial categories, or to gender, or to neither? Are our strategies militant street theater or professional public relations? Do we form coalitions? With whom?

The integration of sexual orientation antidiscrimination laws into the legal text of a community can have tremendous symbolic value. Apart from symbolism, however, these laws exist as law. They are rules in the rule of law. They have force and are enforceable. As such, they raise important issues for any lesbian legal theory.

These issues revolve around the confusion of force with power, specifically our empowerment. No ordinance will empower us. What such an ordinance will do is penalize others who discriminate against us on the basis of our lesbianism, and in some cases we will be compensated with money for this discrimination. We must prove the discrimination that we suffer with reference to a heterosexual norm. We exist in the discourse of discrimination as victims, as deviants.

The discourse of discrimination measures us not only against a heterosexual norm, but against each other. If a company employs four lesbians, a new manager can fearlessly fire the one who has her nose pierced or is the most outspoken or who walks the dykiest. The remaining three lesbians insulate the company from charges of discrimination on the basis of lesbianism. Antidiscrimination is thus partial, allowing the selection of only the whitest and brightest of us, the ones with the best clothes and accents, the smoothest legs and apolitical pasts.

Another danger in the discourse of discrimination is the domestication of our experiences into narratives constructed by the rules of law rather than ourselves. Legal discrimination needs evidence: direct statements, outrageous incidents, statistics. As many lesbians who have experienced discrimination on the basis of race, gender, age, handicap, and nationality know, the laws prohibiting such discrimination often produce civility and subterfuge rather than equality. The statements will be ambiguous, the incidents banal, and the numbers innocent. We can internalize the law and convince ourselves that we are not really being discriminated against because we do not meet the legal criteria.

The law is a limited remedy for our marginalization. This is not to say that we should not press forward with legal reform; that we should not lobby and vote for national, state, and local antidiscrimination laws that include lesbianism; that we should not litigate for judicial interpretations that protect lesbianism. Such efforts can assist with our daily survival as well as our survival as lesbians. But the danger is that we will confuse reform with revolution, and remedying the marginalizations that occur to all lesbians requires nothing less than revolution.

Such revolution is not necessarily legally based. We may experience ourselves as marginalized when we take law as the center. If we put lesbians at the center, however, a different impression of the legal discourse of discrimination results. Imagine a national lesbian conference intended for lesbians only. Imagine a civil suit brought by a heterosexual married couple on the basis of an antidiscrimination law that includes sexual orientation. Imagine an injunction, a court order requiring the lesbian conference to allow Mr. and Mrs. (as she prefers to be denominated) X to attend. Imagine Mr. X speaking out at the lesbian battering workshop, the sober dykes workshop, the separatists' workshop. Imagine Mrs. X handing out leaflets that denounce lesbianism, sex outside of marriage, fatherless households.

This scenerio is not far-fetched, either factually or legally. At the National Lesbian Conference held in Atlanta in 1990, there were rumors that a gay male-owned enterprise had originally been denied space in the "Lesbian Marketplace," had threatened legal action on the basis of discrimination, and had been afforded space. What interests me about this rumor is not its truth, but multitudes of conversations fueled by the signs in the marketplace that read, *Don't assume you are buying from a lesbian,* and at a few booths, *Assume I'm a lesbian.* These conversations generally acknowledged the rule of law as nondiscriminatory but unfair, although many lesbians apologized for this seeming contradiction. The signs attempted to reclaim the power of discrimination. A few journalists decried lesbian attempts to exclude nonlesbians as hypocritical—a discriminatory stance that was intolerable when taken by those who seek nondiscrimination from the dominant culture.

The dominant culture's legal rules support the position that discrimination is abstract and unconnected to other power relations. For example, the Wisconsin antidiscrimination statutory scheme that many consider a lesbian and gay rights model explicitly defines sexual orientation as "having a preference for heterosexuality, homosexuality or bisexuality."[6] While inclusion of the heterosexual preference does have a leveling effect, it also legally prohibits lesbian-only events. The Wisconsin statute is not unique. The current condition of discrimination discourse privileges equality over specific advantages for historically marginalized groups. So-called reverse discrimination is well established within the law. In the education area, for example, the United States Supreme Court has held that a white man has a claim of discrimination against a state university that allocated a certain percentage of seats for "minority" applicants, and that a white man has a claim of discrimination against a state university that was exclusively for women.[7] When we theorize from a place where lesbians are at the center, the discourse of discrimination may not be what we desire.

Equality and antidiscrimination, however weakened and perverted during the last decade, remain the most sacred rules of law to many lesbians. But we must critically examine them. The law's assumption of equalities of power (or more cynically, its indifference to such equalities) poses problems for lesbians. Ultimately, the question we must face is whether we are willing to trade having lesbians in the Girl Scouts for having Mr. and Mrs. X at lesbian events. For those lesbians who judge this an undesirable trade, the challenge becomes reconceptualizing the discourse of discrimination under the rule of law.

A larger challenge is developing our own discourse. Equality as expressed in antidiscrimination laws domesticates us, marginalizes us, and victimizes us. It domesticates us when we discredit our own experiences of marginalization and victimization because we do not fit the legal criteria. Yet these legal strategies can also afford concrete improvements as we live our lives within the dominant culture. They can even make us validate our own experiences because they have been recognized by the law.

Within our own communities, theories, and relationships, the implementation of equality in the form of antidiscrimination rules of law would bring out change. Gone would be the Latina Lesbian Caucus, women-only space, sliding scales, anthologies of older lesbians. If we accepted the rule of law as the rule of lesbianism, we would not discriminate between lesbians and nonlesbians. For many of us, this is unacceptable.

I am not proposing that we must either totally adopt antidiscrimination discourse into all facets of our lives, or we must totally abandon it as a legal strategy. Such a duality is a false one. We are not hypocritical, inconsistent, or contradictory if we recognize antidiscrimination as a potential strategy for legal change, yet recognize its limitations. Our desires are as complex as we are. Concepts such as equality and antidiscrimination cannot fulfill our desires. Yet we can use these legal notions to effect the type of legal change that can facilitate our survival. Our formidable task is strategizing, theorizing, and actualizing our own desires against a legal background of discrimination, all the while resisting our own domestication.

ENDNOTES

1. For one of the most nuanced arguments, see Elvira Morales Arriola, *Sexual Identity and the Constitution: Homosexual Persons as a Discrete and Insular Minority,* 10 WOMEN'S RIGHTS LAW REPORTER 143 (1988).

2. BenShalom v. Marsh, 881 F.2d 456, 464 (7th Cir. 1989). The case involved a lesbian Army reservist; lesbians in the military are further discussed in chapter 7.

3. See Howard Winant, *Postmodern Racial Politics: Difference and Inequality,* 46/7 THE SOCIALIST REVIEW 121 (1990).

4. For example, see chapter 10 discussing the court's treatment of equal protection challenges to marriage as limited to heterosexual couples.

5. Curran v. Mount Diablo Council of the Boy Scouts of America, 147 Cal. App. 3d 712, 195 Cal. Rptr. 325 (1983).

6. WI. Stat. §111.32 (13m).

7. See Mississippi University for Women v. Hogan, 458 U.S. 718 (1982); Regents of the University of California v. Bakke, 438 U.S. 265 (1978).

7

LESBIANS AND THE MILITARY

Perhaps nowhere is the task of strategizing, theorizing, and actualizing lesbian desires more formidable than in the military context. The image of lesbians in the military and related government service raises many contradictions, especially for lesbians active in antimilitarism and antigovernment movements. Yet the military and government services remain the United States' largest employer.

Generally, the consideration of employment discrimination begins with an analysis of whether the employer can be categorized as public or private. This categorical distinction is important because public and governmental employers usually afford employees more rights against discrimination, wrongful termination, and failure to hire. For lesbians, however, the public/private employer distinction is a distinction without a difference, except perhaps for the power of the military and other public employers to enact their discriminatory policies into law.

While private employers rarely enunciate explicit policies that exclude lesbians,[1] the United States Department of Defense has an express policy codified as a rule of law. According to the current Code of Federal Regulations, "Homosexuality is incompatible with military service. The presence in the military environment of persons who engage in homosexual conduct seriously impairs the military mission."[2] The Code offers the rationales for this exclusionary policy as the maintenance of discipline and morale, the lack of privacy among service members who must live in close proximity, the need for public acceptability of the military, and the prevention of breaches of security. The Code mandates "separation" from the military in instances of homosexuality, including when the service member has engaged in, attempted, or solicited any homosexual act, when the service member has stated that she is a homosexual, and when the service member has attempted to marry a person of the same biological sex.[3]

The current forms of these exclusionary regulations are attributable to the efforts of lesbian Army Reserve Sergeant Miriam Ben-Shalom. Ben-Shalom successfully challenged the prior rule of law that allowed discharge for a lesbian who "evidenced homosexual tendencies, desire or interest, but is without overt sexual acts." Because the only evidence against Miriam Ben-Shalom was her own statement that she was a lesbian, she argued that the regulation violated her constitutional rights to free speech. A federal trial court agreed and ordered Ben-Shalom be reinstated. Interestingly, the Army did not appeal the trial court's order; it simply failed to comply with it. Ben-Shalom again sued the Army, and the Army ultimately complied. Yet although she had been reinstated, the Army subsequently denied her a routine reenlistment. By this time, the federal regulation had been changed, and the Army successfully argued that Ben-Shalom could be barred from reenlistment under the new regulation. A United States appellate court found that the new regulation was constitutional and that Miriam Ben-Shalom's constitutional rights to free speech were not being infringed: She "can say what she wants to about homosexuals, but if plaintiff [Ben-Shalom] admits that she is one, then the Army has the right to say something in response, and that is that she is therefore not acceptable in the armed forces."[4] The army's action in denying Ben-Shalom employment is equated with speech.

A similar case is that of Dusty Pruitt, recommended for discharge by the Army because of an article in the *L.A. Times* profiling her as a lesbian Army Reserve chaplain and captain who had had a commitment ceremony with a woman. Pruitt sued, alleging her constitutional rights to free speech were infringed. Although this claim, too, was unsuccessful, it may, in fact, turn out to be viable. The appellate court in Pruitt took a broader perspective than their counterpart in Miriam Ben-Shalom's case. They held that the Army must at least make a showing of the rational basis for the regulation. While the court did not adopt the construction of lesbians as a suspect class, as discussed in the last chapter, the court at least demanded the rationale be more than a mere statement that the Army had a right to have whatever policy it desired.[5]

Miriam Ben-Shalom and Dusty Pruitt are just two of the hundreds of lesbians discharged from the military. In 1987 alone, 244 women were discharged for lesbianism. In proportion to their numbers, women are more likely to be discharged for violating the regulation prohibiting homosexuality than are men; estimates range from three to four times more likely to ten times more likely. This disparity is explained by some in terms of the prevalent misogyny of the military and the use of lesbian-baiting to control all women.[6]

Another explanation offered is the military's deployment of a different strategy to discover lesbianism. The military is reputed for its purges or "witch hunts" of lesbians, and among the branches of the military, the Marine Corps is the most notorious. The witch hunt appellation is appropriate given the tactic of isolating accused women and pressuring them to reveal the names of other lesbians in return for a less severe punishment for themselves. Another tactic is to discourage women from testifying on behalf of each other, lest they be accused themselves or otherwise punished.

The Marine investigation of women at Parris Island 1986-1988 is perhaps the best known of these purges. Of the 246 women at this recruit training depot, almost half were interrogated. Many of these women chose to resign rather than endure further investigation. Twenty-seven women were discharged. Three women received prison sentences, pay forfeitures, reductions in rank, and dishonorable discharges. On appeal in the courts of military review, the convictions were reversed because of military bias as a result of overzealous prosecution. At the trial of Barbara Baum, two of the court martial members had participated in the investigation. By the time the military review court judged this as inappropriate, Barbara Baum had served 226 days of her sentence.[7] At the trial of Cheryl Jameson, two women who testified on her behalf were relieved of their positions, and other potential witnesses were admonished not to testify. The military review court found this constituted unlawful command influence and remanded the case for a new trial.[8] Glenda Jones entered a negotiated plea, but the military review court found this conviction was tainted by the command influence exerted in the previous Jameson trial.[9]

The penalties imposed on the lesbian Marines from Parris Island are present-day anomalies, although they were once standard operating procedure. The effect of a dishonorable discharge is akin to a felony conviction; it limits the prospect of future employment. Any employment with a governmental agency is unlikely and often prohibited, including with agencies unrelated to the military such as the post office, school systems, and public libraries. Many private companies will also refuse to employ anyone dishonorably discharged. Discharge status is a common question on employment applications.

Recent policy changes have resulted in more than half of the separations made on the basis of sexuality being characterized as honorable.[10] Nevertheless, even an honorable discharge means being fired. Although the military can assume a uniquely powerful status, it is still an employer like any other in terms of providing the means for daily survival. Many lesbians who join the military do so to insure their economic survival as well as undertake a secure career. The exclusion of a lesbian from the military can deny her subsistence.

Recognition that the military can contribute to the economic survival of lesbians is one reason for reform of the rule of law that excludes lesbians from the military. One moderate suggestion is to change the exclusion from its present mandatory nature to a more discretionary one—allowing commanders and service secretaries to have the discretion to retain lesbians upon a determination that the lesbian "has value to the military."[11] The broader reform would abolish the exclusion totally. Advocates of the latter also base their advocacy—at least in part—upon the value of lesbians to the military. Much quoted is a once-secret memo from a military officer that described lesbians as "hard-working, career-oriented, willing to put in long hours and among the command's best professionals."[12] Thus, it seems that the military not only supports lesbians, but lesbians support the military.

The portrait of the lesbian as exemplary soldier is troubling. As a military review court in the case of Parris Island Marine Cheryl Jameson noted: "The armed forces would likely be immobilized if they confined themselves to relying for the accomplishment of their diverse missions exclusively upon those who subjectively agreed with all their policies. The success of great military campaigns depends upon the willingness of subordinates at all levels to carry out everything from minute tasks to broad aims and strategies with which they do not necessarily agree, and it may also require them actively to suppress the disagreement of others, or even to feign their own agreement, therewith in the interest of fostering unity of purpose and action."[13] Such conformist compliancy is antithetical to the exercise of any independent lesbian thought. Being willing to carry out the aims of others—aims which at the very best are uninformed by lesbianism and at the worst are violently hostile toward lesbianism—adversely affects lesbian survival. Being willing to suppress the disagreement of other lesbians in favor of a military campaign subordinates lesbian survival to military survival.

The *good soldier* then becomes a category that we attempt to argue ourselves into, as if this will make us more acceptable and less lesbian. Acceptability, compliance, and being a good soldier often means becoming "cannon fodder" and encouraging other lesbians to do the same. Even intensely patriotic and promilitary lesbians like Mary Ann Humphrey, author of *My Country, My Right to Serve,* conclude that the "military has been much like a fickle lover, embracing gays[/lesbians] and other minorities as welcome cannon fodder when there is a need for maximum manpower."[14] Her remedy of making the military a more consistent lover, welcoming lesbians even in periods of "limited action and peacetime," does not necessarily dispel the notion of lesbians as expendable.

Because the military's class system cannot be divorced from American hierarchies such as race and class, other disenfranchised groups as well as lesbians of the lowest ranks and lowest classes are considered the most expendable. While women in the military are a small percentage of total soldiers (ranging from 5-13 percent in various branches), of these women a disproportionate number are women of color (ranging from 27-50 percent in various branches). The unfairness of the present exclusion of lesbians and gay men is often analogized to the previous racial segregation in the military. This analogy is supported by the military's rationale of cohesion, image, and authority in both situations.

While lesbian exclusion is the present rule of law, lesbian inclusion could be mandated by law. Apart from the financial coercion that renders the military a good occupation given the range of other economic opportunities available, and the ideological coercion that romanticizes the military as a vehicle for foreign travel rather than armed terror, there is the possibility of conscription. To date, this has not been an historical reality for women. The United States Supreme Court rejected a claim in the early 1980s that the Congressional decision to exempt women from registering for the draft violated (men's) equal protection. The Court reasoned that because Congress had also excluded women from combat duty, Congress could also exclude women from mandatory draft registration because they were not "similarly situated" to combat-eligible men.[15] However, Congress has recently removed the combat exclusion for women, allowing them to serve in combat positions during the Gulf War. Although Congress has always had the ability to require women to register for the draft and to draft women, courts would now have a difficult time upholding a Congressional decision not to conscript combat-eligible women. Interestingly, one of the most common arguments against the ERA was that it would have required the drafting of women.

The drafting of women, like the drafting of men, has class and race dimensions. Exemptions, like those for educational status, are often class-based. The racism of draft practices is generally acknowledged and is illustrated by the case of Perry Watkins. When Watkins received a draft notice during the Vietnam War, he returned it with a check in the *yes* box for "homosexual tendencies" because he knew he was gay. The Army sent him to a psychiatrist who engaged in explicit conversations with Watkins concerning his preferences and practices of gay male sex. Nevertheless, the psychiatrist certified Watkins as not gay. Watkins recalls that every gay white person he knew who marked the form similarly was not inducted, but as a Black gay male he was.

Perry Watkins requested numerous discharges because of his gayness during his time in the Army. He was always denied. Ultimately, Watkins made a career of the military, a career that included such official duties as entertaining while dressed in drag. After fifteen years of service, the military turned down a routine reenlistment based upon his sexuality. Watkins sued the Army and prevailed on an estoppel theory, meaning that because the Army knew that he was gay from the very beginning of his career, the Army was estopped from taking negative action on that basis at this late date, five years short of a retirement that would provide him with a substantial pension.[16] The Watkins case is one of the very few in which the highest court to hear the case did not capitulate to the military. Like the deference accorded to prison administrators discussed in chapter 9, judicial deference to the military is enshrined in the rule of law. In this way, the rule of law becomes the rule of the military.

As lesbians, we must resist becoming domesticated by the rule of law's deference to the military. If our refusal to defer includes the centering of lesbian concerns rather than military ones, arguments that lesbians make good soldiers become superfluous. The inquiry becomes, instead, whether soldiers make good lesbians. We need to decide for ourselves what makes a good lesbian and think about our own desires for our individual and collective lesbian survival. Obviously, a dead lesbian is not a good lesbian. To the extent that military service is linked to lesbian deaths, it is hostile to our survival at the most elemental level.

The rule of law exemplified by the rule of the military confines us within our "domestic" borders. This confinement is enforced through the ideology of patriotism. Lesbians who are not sufficiently patriotic will be terrorized in the military not only because of their lesbianism, but because of their "radical politics."[17] Love for the patria—the fatherland—supercedes our love for ourselves. Any commitment to collective lesbian survival is subordinated to a commitment to national survival. The survival of a nation founded to protect the interests of nonlesbians. The survival of a nation codifying its violence toward lesbian existence in its rules of law. Lesbian survival is secondary, at best.

Of course, as lesbians we each have national and cultural identities, but our own identities are not necessarily consistent with legal geographical boundaries. For example, a lesbian may consider herself Appalachian, rather than West Virginian or even American. Nationalism, as enforced by the rule of law, supports not only our own domestication, but the domestication—and destruction—of other lesbians. This is not consistent with lesbian survival. When a lesbian officer in the United States Army trains a lesbian recruit to think of current unpopular foreigners as "enemies," she is training one lesbian to hate another. The military is directly responsible for the death of many lesbians, the rape of others, and limiting the survival for lesbian existence. To disregard the survival of lesbians because they live within the national boundaries of Korea, Vietnam, El Salvador, Nicaragua, or Iraq is to disregard the survival of lesbians. The military's purpose is war. The changing of the name from the Department of War to the Department of Defense masks, but does not alter, the purpose. The (non)labeling of the deaths of lesbians as general casualties obscures but does not prevent lesbian deaths.

I am not suggesting that lesbianism mandates pacifism. I do believe, however, that the allegiance to nation demanded by the military is ultimately inconsistent with lesbian survival. And I am suggesting that lesbianism, as love for women, is inconsistent with a belief that some women should be killed because of conflicts between nations.

Nevertheless, the rule of law's current explicit exclusion of lesbians from military employment domesticates us—even those of us not in the military—by the force of its judgment that lesbianism is not acceptable. It is yet another rule of law exhibiting violence toward us. The military exclusion domesticates all of us in another way as well: its very explicitness keeps us riveted. We direct our efforts toward the abolition of the exclusion, rather than adopting a broader agenda.

Many people are expending impressive energies agitating for this abolition—in the courts, in Congress, and through military channels. These efforts receive extensive coverage in the lesbian/gay press. The revelation of secret Pentagon documents recommending a policy reversal, and the announcement of the gay identity of the assistant secretary of defense for public affairs, has contributed to coverage in the mainstream press as well. Even *Time* magazine wanted to know, in a way that begged the question, whether a volunteer armed forces could afford to exclude talented people.[18] Many are predicting that the exclusion will be abolished in the near future, just as the explicit immigration exclusion (see chapter 8) was recently abolished.

A large portion of the solicitation mail I have received lately has been seeking my support for efforts to abolish the explicit military exclusion. But when I read the boldface telling me I am a known patriot, I am distressed. And when I see the red type urging me to prove my patriotism by my contribution, I am anxious. To the extent that I support other lesbians because of the rule of law's imposition of "nation" and an ideology of patriotism, I am domesticated.

Instead, I believe the exclusion must be abolished because it is detrimental to the lives of real lesbians. Accepting the reality that the military can and does provide the means of economic survival for many lesbians does not necessarily mean we must accept the terms of economic survival as it is constructed by patriarchal powers, including the military, and enforced by the rule of law. When we are domesticated, we do not challenge the conditions of poverty, abuse of women, and racism that make the military an attractive option. When we are domesticated, we do not challenge the differentials in salary, health care, and retirement benefits of child-care workers, construction workers, sales clerks, and craft workers as compared with those of military workers. When we are domesticated, we think such challenges are unrealistic.

The explicit exclusion of lesbians from military service is only the tip of the iceberg. Discrimination exists not only here, but in related quasi-military government agencies like the FBI and the CIA, where lesbians are considered security risks. The military is unique, however, in that it is the ultimate enforcer of the rule of law. As one legal theorist noted, we do not read United States Supreme Court opinions because they are interesting theoretical positions, but because they are backed up by the United States Army.[19] The rule of law the military enforces is a rule of law that often makes us outlaws, seeks to domesticate us, and does not center lesbian survival.

ENDNOTES

1. One exception is the explicit policy of CRACKER BARREL restaurants which provides that it is inconsistent with the chain's "traditional family values" to employ any persons who "fail to demonstrate normal heterosexual values." Some religious employers also have explicit policies.

2. 32 C.F.R. Pt 41, App. A, Pt. 1 H.1.a. (1991).

3. 32 C.F.R. Pt 41, App. A., Pt. 1 H.1.c.

4. Ben-Shalom v. Marsh, 881 F.2d 454, 462 (7th Cir. 1989).

5. Pruitt v. Cheney, 943 F.2d 989 (9th Cir. 1991).

6. For an excellent discussion, see Michele Beneke and Kirstin Dodge, *Military Women in Nontraditional Job Fields: Casualties of the Armed Forces War on Homosexuals*, 13 HARVARD WOMEN'S L. J. 215 (1990).

7. United States v. Baum, 30 M.J. 626 (1990).

8. United States v. Jameson, 33 M.J. 669 (1991).

9. United States v. Jones, 33 M.J. 1040 (1991).

10. Government Document PERS-TR-89-002 (December 1988).

11. Jeffrey Davis, *Military Policy Toward Homosexuals: Scientific, Historical, and Legal Perspectives*, 131 MILITARY L. REV. 55, 105 (1991).

12. The memo is from Admiral Joseph Donnell, Commander of the Navy's Surface Atlantic Fleet. The memo is quoted in the March 15, 1991 letter from Gerry Studds and other Congress persons to President Bush supporting lesbians and gay men in the military.

13. 33 M.J. at 675.

14 MARY ANN HUMPHREY, MY COUNTRY, MY RIGHT TO SERVE at xiii (1990). For discussion of lesbians (and gay men) in World War Two, see ALLEN BERUBE, COMING OUT UNDER FIRE: A HISTORY OF GAY MEN AND WOMEN IN WORLD WAR TWO (1990).

15. Rostker v. Goldberg, 453 U.S. 57 (1981).

16. Watkins v. United States Army, 875 F.2d 699 (9th Cir. 1989) (en banc). Watkin's views of his situation are expressed in HUMPHREY, *supra* note 14 at 248-257.

17. "Again, this was the early fifties and there were witch hunts all over the place. But it wasn't only for lesbianism, it was also for those involved in radical politics— whatever that was. If you weren't a Republican, you were considered a crazy woman." Statements by pseudonymous "Pat Richardson," in *Id.* at 158.

18. *Marching Out of The Closet*, TIME 14, 16 (August 1991).

19. These remarks were made by legal scholar Robert Cover. See generally, Robert Cover, *Violence and the Word*, 95 YALE LAW JOURNAL 1601 (1986).

8

LESBIANS AND IMMIGRATION

The rule of law's domestication of us within national boundaries is the basis not only of militarism, but of immigration. The legal category *good soldier* is only an intensified version of the legal category *citizen*. The American rule of law has specific provisions regulating travel and settlement in the United States depending upon variables like our place of birth and our parents' citizenship status. Other countries also have immigration and sometimes emigration policies articulated in their particular rules of law.

The United States Immigration and Naturalization Service (INS) is the federal agency charged by law with enforcing the federal statutes regulating immigration. The federal statute regulating the INS long mandated that the INS exclude lesbians. Effective June 21, 1991, this explicit exclusion is no longer part of the law. The Immigration Act of 1990 amended the exclusion, which now applies to persons who have been determined:

> (I) to have a physical or mental disorder and behavior associated with the disorder that may pose, or has posed, a threat to the property, safety, or welfare of alien others, or (II) to have had a physical or mental disorder and a history of behavior associated with

the disorder, which behavior has posed a threat to the property, safety, or welfare of the alien or others and which behavior is likely to reoccur or lead to other harmful behavior.[1]

The House of Representatives report prepared in conjunction with the passage of this provision makes it clear that lesbianism is not covered and is not considered a threat to safety, property, or welfare. The House report also references the confusing and contradictory history of the exclusion of lesbians that had been part of the rule of law since 1919. The Immigration and Nationality Act of 1965, in effect until the Act of 1990, expressed the lesbian exclusion as affecting "aliens afflicted with a psychopathic personality, sexual deviation, or a mental defect." The previous act only mentioned psychopathic personalities. However, both sexual deviancy and psychopathic personalities were intended to encompass all homosexuals. Congressional notes referred to the intended exclusion of homosexuals, and the United States Supreme Court found such an exclusion was proper.[2]

From its beginnings, the lesbian exclusion was a result of a partnership between the rule of law and the mandate of the medical establishment. The exclusion was a medical exclusion. As such, the INS was legally required to obtain a medical certificate from the Public Health Service (PHS) in order to exclude lesbian aliens. The medical establishment, however, eventually defected from the partnership. In 1979, then Surgeon General Julius Richmond declared that homosexuality per se was no longer considered a mental disease or defect. This declaration was based on a desire to conform PHS practices to current medical views. He also advised the INS that the PHS would no longer issue medical certificates for those suspected of being "homosexual."

The INS subsequently issued new guidelines and procedures for excluding lesbians. These prohibited INS inspectors from asking aliens entering the country about their sexual preference during the primary inspection. However, if a person should volunteer information regarding her lesbianism during that inspection, or if another alien entering at the same time identified a woman as a lesbian, the INS could ask that person to sign a statement that she was a "homosexual" and could then exclude her.

Advocates across the country challenged these practices and the exclusions of alien lesbians/gay men. One basis of challenge was the INS practice of exclusion without the necessary medical certificate from PHS. Within the same month in 1983, two different federal appellate courts issued contradictory opinions regarding the necessity of this certificate.[3] The United States Supreme Court refused to resolve the conflict.[4]

With these contradictory decisions in the judicial arena, advocates turned to Congressional and administrative lobbying. Ultimately, such efforts were successful. The new act means that the INS is no longer empowered to exclude lesbians on the basis of their lesbianism. The successful struggle for the abolition of the lesbian exclusion in the immigration context is concrete encouragement for the advocates involved in similar intensive efforts to abolish the military's lesbian exclusion. Nevertheless, like the military's explicit exclusion, the INS former exclusion was only the tip of an iceberg. Again like the military, immigration is predicated on national boundaries. Immigration laws enforce these national boundaries.

It is the purpose of the INS to exclude aliens who are not desirable. Desirability is determined with reference to domestic policies. Exclusions take the form of denial of visas, denial of permanent resident status, denial of naturalized citizenship, and deportation. The removal of lesbians from the list of *per se* undesirables still permits lesbians to be excluded for being otherwise threatening to property or safety, being a drug abuser or addict, being convicted of or admitting to crimes of moral turpitude or crimes involving drugs.

In addition to exclusion, lesbians can also suffer nonadmission. Because the government receives more requests for admission into the United States than it has decided it will grant, it employs a system of preferences. These preferences articulate the basis on which applicants are measured in terms of their desirability. The most pervasive preference concerns family relationships, based on the domestic desirability of family unity. Marriage to a United States citizen is accorded great preference. Such a preference rarely applies to lesbians. We cannot marry our lovers and we are relatively unlikely to be married to men. Given the existence of this preference, at least one commentator has argued that INS should adopt a preference based on domestic partnerships as quasi-marriages.[5] Lesbian and gay advocates are lobbying for this change. The domesticating potential, and the relative benefits of arguing ourselves into the legal categories of marriage and coupledom, are further explored in chapter 10.

Another preference that might not be available to lesbians is the one accorded to those who have served in the United States military. Under this policy, a permanent resident with military service will be accorded preference for naturalization. The military's explicit exclusion of lesbians means that they are legally ineligible for service.

Further, the small percentage of women in the military as compared with men reduces a lesbian's statistical chances of being eligible for this preference.

Preferences for visas also include employment-based preferences for immigrants with "extraordinary ability," or who are "outstanding professors or researchers," or who are executives and managers with multinational corporations. While there are certainly lesbians within such categories, the INS might be less likely to so consider a lesbian if her career is lesbian-focused. For example, a lesbian professor with extraordinary abilities to translate lesbian works from one language to another, who is the executive and manager of a multinational/multicultural lesbian publishing house, might not be considered as having received sufficient national or international acclaim to be within the preferential categories. Her acclaim within international lesbian communities would be inadequate.

Employment-based preferences additionally discriminate in ways that do not necessarily further lesbian interests. If we center all lesbians, then preferences for a professor rather than for a disabled and therefore unemployable lesbian are not only divisive but elitist. This elitism and classism is endemic in the immigration preference system. An historic case demonstrates this tendency, as well as the judicial acceptance of such policies. The Supreme Court interpreted a statutory prohibition against organizations paying for passage for aliens who would come into the country to perform "any kind of labor or service" as inapplicable to a Christian minister from England because the exclusion was meant to apply only to manual laborers and not the "professorial man," especially if the professorial man in question were a minister coming to this "religious country."[6]

This case also demonstrates the inherent goal of the immigration policies of preserving the "purity" of a white Christian America. The racism of immigration policies is perhaps most compellingly demonstrated by the Chinese Exclusion Acts. Acts excluding or limiting certain ethnic groups are common in the history of this country's immigration laws. The immigration quotas presently employed by the United States continue this tradition of racism and classism, as well as the xenophobia which enshrines Western and Christian values. Immigration policies make determinations based upon a lesbian's country of origin. Under the present system, a lesbian from certain countries will be more welcome than a lesbian from other countries. The welcome depends upon the United States' relationship with another government. The lesbian is reduced to her nationality. Such a reduction is domesticating.

Nonentitlement to a preference is often tantamount to exclusion. The preferences operate as rules of law that can domesticate us as we attempt to argue ourselves into categories that were never intended to benefit us. Further, the entire system of preferences domesticates us. It tells us that some lesbians are more desirable than others. Just as lesbians worked toward the elimination of the lesbian exclusion, we need to work toward the expansion of preferences. But we are domesticated if we stop with our request to be included in a preferential system. We need to challenge a system of quotas that operates against lesbians depending upon their country of origin. And even more radically, we need to work toward the elimination of legal categories that privilege the *domestic,* that judge some lesbians *aliens,* and make determinations about whether lesbians can be *naturalized.* Our acceptance of these legal categories and our acceptance of national boundaries ultimately domesticates all of us.

ENDNOTES

1. P.L. 101-649 (1990) to be codified at 8 U.S.C. §1182.

2. Boutilier v. INS, 387 U.S. 118 (1967) (interpreting the 1952 Act).

3. Compare In re Longstaff, 716 F.2d 1439 (5th Cir. 1983) (upholding the exclusion of a gay man from naturalization despite the lack of a medical certificate) with Hill v. INS, 714 F.2d 1470 (9th Cir. 1983) (holding that INS may not exclude a self proclaimed gay man without a medical certificate of sexual deviancy or psychopathic personality).

4. The United States Supreme Court denied a petition for certiorari in Longstaff, 467 U.S. 1219 (1984).

5. Sandra Lundy, *"I Do" But I Can't: Immigration Policy and Gay Domestic Relationships,* 5 YALE LAW AND POLICY REV. 185 (1986).

6. Holy Trinity Church v. United States, 143 U.S. 457 (1892).

9

LESBIANS AND PRISON

The first piece of legal scholarship I undertook concerned the rule of law's recognition of justifications for the crime of escaping from prison. I learned that one justification could be continuous threats from a "group of lesbian inmates" about performing "lesbian acts—the exact expression was 'fuck or fight.' " The California appellate court in this case, *People v. Lovercamp*, distanced itself from the lesbianism involved, confessing "a certain naiveté as to just what kind of exotic erotica is involved in the gang rape of the victim by a group of lesbians and a total ignorance of just who is forced to do what to whom." Nevertheless, the judges found a threatened lesbian attack similar enough to threats of forcible sodomy between men and thus sufficient to constitute a possible defense to an escape from prison. The Lovercamp opinion is a liberal one. Not only does it reverse the trial court's rejection that aggression could be a defense to an escape prosecution, but it also recognizes the fault of prison administrators who condone violence by their inaction. Yet the opinion perpetuates the stereotype of aggressive incarcerated lesbians attacking heterosexual innocents like Marsha Lovercamp, described in the opinion as having "the intelligence of a twelve-year-old." Like the B-movies and pornographic novels that inform the rule of law's perceptions of lesbianism in prison, the Lovercamp opinion circumvents the realities of incarcerated lesbians.[1]

The rule of law has its own justification for its circumvention. Like courts considering military matters, courts considering controversies arising in prison apply a deferential standard. Prison officials are treated as experts entitled to deference. When inmates challenge prison regulations or conditions, prison administrators usually raise security issues, and courts often refuse to interfere. The security claim can be made about lesbian prisoners both as to the security of other prisoners whom the aggressive lesbians might attack, as well as to the lesbian prisoners themselves, potentially in danger from hostile homophobic prisoners. While this security claim is usually relatively effective, in one recent case—resolved without litigation—it was insufficient. A county prison in Florida braceleted, with red bands, women prisoners who revealed their lesbianism in intake interviews. Ten women complained, not only because of the bracelets known as "pink tags," but also because being pink-tagged meant a loss of privileges, such as showers, and an enforcement of segregation from the general prison population. While the prison officials originally attempted to claim security in this case, they withdrew the claim after the braceleting practice was revealed and disparaged. The practice of segregation, however, remains widespread in many prisons.

Another policy justified in terms of security is the censoring of lesbian publications. Like many other constitutional rights, the First Amendment right to free speech and access to publications is restricted in prison. Lesbian publications are sometimes thought to promote rebellion, illegal sexual expression, and antagonism. While publications are not necessarily censored, prison officials are free to inspect particular issues for offensive materials. The availability of lesbian publications is also problematic. Many lesbian, lesbian/gay, and feminist publications announce themselves as free to lesbian prisoners. Yet prison officials often restrict the sharing of reading materials between prisoners, restrict the accumulation of materials (under fire hazard as well as security regulations), and restrict the receipt of such materials to those mailed directly from publishers rather than from private persons.

Perhaps the most totalizing restriction on women prisoners justified in terms of the catchall of security is the often unwritten no-contact rule. A kiss is forbidden; a hug is illegal; even the most casual touch during a conversation can be an infraction. Physical contact can result in a range of disciplinary actions, which include the loss of privileges such as showers, library time, and exercise, as well as written warnings placed in one's file which are reviewed by parole boards and can affect the possibility of parole and the accumulation of release time.

Despite the no-contact rule, lesbian sexual expression and lesbianism exist in prison, perhaps in greater proportion than in non-prison contexts. The very existence of lesbianism is an act of resistance. Nevertheless, lesbianism is variously domesticated, tolerated, and manipulated by the rule of law's total and arbitrary ascendancy in the prison context. The women's prison system often controls prisoners through paternalism and what may be described as the "sororitization" of "our girls."[2] Historically, women's prisons—rather than co-gender institutions—resulted from women reformers who believed in feminine morality, both for the prisoners and the prison administrators. In the context of abuses of women prisoners by male prisoners and male guards who routinely raped the women, assigned them to the status of servants, or at best ignored them, the reform of sex-segregated prisons was a marked advancement. However, sex-segregated prisons became, and remain, a separate sphere in which domesticity is stressed. Lesbianism can be a part of that domesticity, in spite of no-contact rules, as long as it stays within acceptable bounds.

One example of lesbianism beyond the bounds of acceptability is the well-documented incident at the Bedford Hills Reformatory for Women in 1915. Bedford Hills, which is still in existence, was founded as a model in the feminine prison reform movement. Its initial prison administrators tolerated lesbianism and mandated racial integration. Subsequent administrators became embarrassed by an investigation that revealed lesbian attachments between white and black prisoners. Rather than harsher restrictions on lesbianism, however, the prison administrators enforced racial segregation. Lesbianism across the racial divide was lesbianism beyond acceptable bounds.[3]

Contemporary examples of lesbianism that cross acceptable boundaries may transgress a less easily ascertainable kind of divide. This demarcating boundary is between "real" lesbians and "situational" lesbians. Real lesbians are considered women who were lesbians prior to incarceration and who are openly lesbian. Situational lesbians are considered otherwise acceptable women coping with the deprivation of male affection. Comparing these two groups, using indicators such as age of first lesbian sexual experience, one sociological researcher investigating a women's prison in the South concluded that real lesbians were "more criminalistic, more feministic and more aggressive."[4] Such sociological conclusions are reaffirmed as common wisdom in anecdote after anecdote. For example, in the early 1980s I inspected a women's prison as part of a federal court team interested in the total lack of civil rights complaints filed by inmates in the women's prison, especially as compared with the thousands filed by male inmates. When I asked the female prison administrator about prison policies affecting lesbianism, she assumed a condescending tone as she informed me that women isolated from men still needed companionship and affection. However, she was quick to add, there were certain incorrigible lesbians who dominated other women, harassed the guards, flaunted their lifestyles, could not accept discipline, and were troublemakers. She then showed me units where such lesbians were housed until they learned to be more "ladylike"— separate isolation maximum security units that sharply contrasted with the studied campus atmosphere of the rest of the facility. In a more recent example, a life-long lesbian incarcerated at numerous New York prisons reported that correction officers routinely assigned the dirtiest jobs to prisoners who were too openly or outwardly lesbian.[5]

The prison system operates as a microcosm of society in its domestication of lesbianism. The domesticated ladylike discrete lesbian is tolerated; others are not. Interestingly, the ways in which we participate in our own domestication and the domestication of other lesbians is also illustrated by the prison microcosm. Many correctional officers and former prisoners will maintain informally that women correctional officers are disproportionately lesbians. Prison officials will not confirm such statistics, just as they are reluctant to discuss unwritten policies affecting lesbianism among prisoners. However, even a statistically conservative estimate would mean that at least a few correctional officers and prison administrators are lesbians. It is horrific to contemplate even one lesbian correctional officer or prison administrator pursuing disciplinary actions against one lesbian for hugging her lover, or recommending the transfer of one lesbian to another facility away from her lover, or confiscating a lesbian magazine, or taunting an insufficiently demure lesbian. Yet being a correctional officer or prison administrator is viable employment, like being a member of the military. Further, the lesbian correctional officer or prison administrator functions like the lesbian personnel officer at a private company, the lesbian social worker at an adoption agency, the lesbian police officer, the lesbian lawyer. She can be a good guard, employer, social worker, cop, attorney, or a bad one. Either way, she can be an agent of our domestication.

One of the most dangerous ways in which we participate in our own domestication is in our acceptance of the rule of law that judges some lesbians deserving of imprisonment. When we theorize lesbianism and lesbian community, we often exclude the lesbians who have been or are incarcerated or institutionalized.[6] This exclusion is based on the rule of law's judgment about certain lesbians, rather than lesbian judgments. For example, the rule of law will judge a lesbian who exchanges sex for money, or who buys drugs, or who lies to a welfare agency, a criminal and incarcerate her. Lesbian judgments about the relative evils of prostitution, drug use, or welfare fraud might well be different. Moreover, the rule of law's judgments in individual cases may be incorrect. Lesbians who are not guilty of the crime charged may nevertheless be convicted, perhaps because of antilesbian biases on the part of the judge or jury. Or the imprisonment may occur without any conviction. Lesbian Laura Whitehorn remained in "preventative detention" for five years awaiting trial on charges related to her revolutionary activities.[7]

We also domesticate our individual lives with these judgments enforced by the rule of law. We conform our actions so that we are not judged criminal or insane or incompetent or delinquent. The fear of being institutionalized in a prison or other reformatory or rehabilitative institution domesticates us. The fear is a realistic one, of course. State institutions are brutal places in which to attempt to survive. For lesbians with HIV, cancer, or other diseases, the inadequate health care available in state institutions can be a death sentence. For every lesbian, the violent climate in prisons can kill the body as well as the spirit.

The rule of law's divisive violence that domesticates all of us by institutionalizing some of us can appear rational because we have internalized the categories *criminal, incompetent,* and *delinquent.* These categories appear especially rational to us as lesbians when we believe our lesbianism is not the cause of the institutionalization. Even if we agree that criminal sanctions for prostitution, drug use, or welfare fraud are unfair, we can too easily accept the myth that such rules of law are applied to everyone. Yet lesbianism is always implicated in the judgment of any lesbian as criminal, insane, incompetent, or delinquent. Again, a sociological study concludes that as compared with heterosexual women, lesbians "had longer sentences, were arrested at an earlier age, were more likely to have been previously confined, and had served more time."[8] It should not surprise us that the rule of law's enforcement of its criminal codes is homophobic. The racism, classism, and ableism that infect the criminal justice system also contribute to the incarceration of many, many lesbians.

Even when we acknowledge the heterosexism, racism, classism, and ableism endemic to the criminal and quasi-criminal justice system, American lesbians are often self-satisfied when considering the international perspective. In many countries, lesbians (and gay men) are imprisoned for their stated sexual preference or acts of sexual expression. While in the United States lesbians can be imprisoned for acts of lesbian sex, as discussed in chapter 4, the rarity of imprisonment insulates us from confronting our criminal status. Repression in other countries can seem more overt and immediate.[9]

International human rights organizations have generally ignored lesbian repression until quite recently. For example, not until the autumn of 1991 did the largest and most prestigious of these groups, Amnesty International, agree to include lesbians and gay men imprisoned for their claims of sexual preference as well as for sexual expression (if committed in private between consenting adults) as prisoners of conscience. This recognition occurred only after intense and lengthy agitation by many lesbian/gay rights groups, including the International Lesbian Gay Association (ILGA), which has recently gained some status at the United Nations. Nevertheless, ILGA does not yet have official recognition as a human rights agency.

The recognition of international lesbianism and agitation for freedom for all lesbians is vital.[10] We cannot afford to be domesticated by the rule of law's category of *nation* in the prison context any more than in the military or immigration contexts. At the same time, we cannot allow comparative arguments to justify the American rule of law's division of lesbians into those deserving of institutionalization and those deserving of relative freedom.

ENDNOTES

1. People v. Lovercamp, 43 Cal. App. 3d 823, 118 Cal. Rptr. 110 (1974).

2. Cynthia Serrano, attorney at the Prisoners' Rights Project, as interviewed by Guljit Bains.

3. ESTELLE B. FREEDMAN, THEIR SISTERS' KEEPERS: WOMEN'S PRISON REFORM IN AMERICA, 1830-1930 at 139-141 (1981). I owe much of my understanding of the history of women's prisons to Estelle Freedman's excellent book.

See also, NICOLE HAHN RAFTER, PARTIAL JUSTICE: WOMEN IN STATE PRISONS, 1800-1935 (1985).

4. Robert Leger, *Lesbianism Among Women Prisoners: Participants and Nonparticipants,* 14:4 CRIMINAL JUSTICE AND BEHAVIOR 448 (1987).

5. Anonymous forty-two-year-old lesbian previously incarcerated at Bedford Hills, Albion and Taconic, interviewed by Guljit Bains.

6. I first heard the argument that lesbians in prison must be part of our communities articulated by Judy Greenspan, whose work with the National Prison Project of the ACLU has done much to advance the causes of lesbian and gay prisoners.

7. See Susie Day, *Lesbian Political Prisoners,* OUT/WEEK (November 5, 1989).

8. Robert Leger, *supra* note 4.

9. For an excellent discussion of the international legal status of lesbianism, see the SECOND ILGA PINK BOOK (1988).

10. For an excellent guide to international lesbian groups, see SHELLEY ANDERSON, OUT IN THE WORLD: INTERNATIONAL LESBIAN ORGANIZING (Ithaca, New York: Firebrand Books 1991).

LESBIAN RELATIONSHIPS

10

LESBIANS AS LOVERS

Ⓐll of the criminalization, discrimination, and regulation discussed in the previous chapters is targeted at preventing lesbian relationships. We call each other lovers, friends, sisters, compañeras. We are coupled or not, sexual or not, cohabitating or not. But whatever we are, we are not legal.

The rules of law that are the rules of men do not include a rule honoring lesbian relationships. What makes this exclusion important are the rules of law that reenforce other relationships. At times, lesbian relationships suffer by comparison: a lesbian couple in which one lover has paid employment and the other does not is excluded from benefits regarding taxes, insurance, and other economic matters that the rules of law guarantee for a legally married couple in the same situation. At other times, lesbian relationships suffer more directly: a member of a lesbian couple who becomes incapacitated can be controlled by a person determined in accordance with relationships recognized under the rule of law, such as the father who does not believe she is a lesbian, the brother who abused her, or the husband she has not seen for twenty years but never divorced. The exclusion of our relationships from the realm of legal recognition affects our lesbian survival both comparatively and directly.

When we think of the potential for horror in the law's non-recognition of our relationships, we think of Sharon Kowalski and Karen Thompson. In November of 1983, Sharon Kowalski was in a car accident and suffered extensive physical and neurological injuries limiting, among other things, her ability to communicate. She had been living, until her accident, with her lover Karen Thompson, in a house they were buying together. After her accident, Sharon could not be self-sufficient, and the question became who would be responsible for her care. Despite the fact that she and Karen had exchanged rings and considered their relationship a "life partnership, similiar to a marriage," they were legally strangers. Relationships by marriage or blood are the legally privileged ones. In Sharon's case, the rule of law gave first preference to her parents, parents who did not believe that their daughter was a lesbian or could be involved in a lesbian relationship with anyone, including Karen Thompson. If the law judged Sharon's parents as guardians—the persons legally responsible for Sharon—Sharon's parents could not only control Sharon's finances and medical treatment choices, but also determine where Sharon would live and who could visit her. The prospect of not being allowed to even visit with her lover prompted Karen Thompson to bring an action in court. In one of the many court papers filed in the litigation, a doctor testifying on behalf of Sharon's parents stated that "visits by Karen Thompson would expose Sharon Kowalski to a high risk of sexual abuse."[1]

Such homophobic statements, coupled with the feelings of many lesbian lovers that they were only a car accident away from Karen and Sharon's situation, contributed to the attention the case was able to attract. Lesbian, as well as gay, bisexual, feminist, and disability activists focused considerable energies on the litigation. In eight years of court proceedings, Karen Thompson won many battles, including the right to visit her lover. Finally, in December 1991, a Minnesota appellate court ordered that she be appointed guardian. The case is presently being appealed.

The history of the case is illuminating. Despite the fact that Sharon's parents withdrew their claim to be their daughter's guardian, the original judge refused to name Karen Thompson as guardian. The trial judge expressed concerns that Sharon's parents still objected to Karen as guardian (in part on the basis of her lesbianism), that Karen has been involved with at least one other woman in the years since Sharon's 1983 accident, and that Karen invaded Sharon's privacy by revealing her sexual orientation to her parents and by taking her to lesbian and gay gatherings. Rather than naming Karen as guardian, the trial judge named a supposedly neutral third party, a legal stranger—not Sharon's lesbian lover.

The appellate court reversed the trial judge's decision. The court relied on the uncontroverted medical testimony that Sharon Kowalski had sufficient capacity to choose her guardian and had consistently chosen Karen Thompson. The court also noted that Karen Thompson was "the only person willing to take care of Sharon Kowalski outside of an institution." In a phrase that the lesbian and gay press reiterated in tones of victory, the appellate court also confirmed the trial court's finding that Sharon and Karen were a "family of affinity which should be accorded respect." This respect, however, is somewhat mitigated by the court's common sense approach in preventing its ward, Sharon, from becoming financially dependent on the state for institutional care.[2]

Because of the Kowalski case, lesbian (and gay) legal reformers have developed strategies to make the rules of law more hospitable to our daily needs. These strategies include both working within the rules of law as they presently exist and efforts to change the rules. This chapter discusses both types of strategies as they affect adult lesbian relationships, while the next chapter discusses relationships with children.

Yet the strategies have not merely been aimed at improving lesbian daily survival. The law also operates on a symbolic level. Regarding our relationships, the law's symbolism is often confusing, contradictory, and pernicious. The *family* is a legal category, but it is the legal category with which we are most intimate. As such, when we think about lesbian relationships, we often evoke family images in a way that blends the intimate and the legal.

It is this blending that has the potential to most severely domesticate our relationships. Our legal arguments that our lover is a *spouse equivalent*, or that our relationship is like a *contract*, potentially extend outside legal forums and into our self-conceptions. The threat is not assimilation, but the unthinking assimilation of domestication. I believe that any lesbian who has thought about marriage and decided that her particular lover is really equivalent to a spouse is making lesbian choices. I believe that any lesbian who has filled out forms describing her lover as a spouse equivalent and then adopts this conception without further thought is making nonlesbian choices.

The challenge is making the law serve lesbian relationships instead of having lesbian relationships serve the law. I began thinking about specific instances of the legal domestication of all lesbian relationships in the context of a specific lesbian relationship. My lover and I had long conversations that sometimes seemed like arguments.

We argued ourselves into writing the law review article cited at the end of this chapter. We eventually reached some agreements, and we divided our judgments into three parts: legal tools to prevent laws that would otherwise operate, contracts, and marriagelike arrangements. I continue to rely upon the three-part division that we developed because it puts lesbians at the center, rather than law, and because it makes distinctions between using law within our relationships and using law with regard to nonlesbians.

Legal Tools of Prevention

Legal workers devoted energy toward developing legal strategies that might prevent Karen and Sharon's situation from happening to others. The legal strategy most often advised, and the one Karen Thompson recommends in her book as well as in her many public speeches, is a legal document called a durable power of attorney.

A durable power of attorney is nothing more than a piece of paper that conforms to some formalities (like witnesses, for example) and authorizes one person to act for another. Traditional powers of attorney generally terminate when the principal—the person who makes the power of attorney—becomes incapacitated. On the other hand, durable powers of attorney generally begin when the principal becomes incapacitated. These durable powers of attorney can authorize one person to make all types of financial decisions, and generally act as an "attorney in fact" for the other. Medical durable powers of attorney can authorize one person to make all types of medical decisions, and generally act as if guardian for the other.

All durable powers of attorney are creatures of state statutes, and so one must research the rules of law in the state in which one lives to determine whether such statutes exist, and if they do, whether there are any limitations. It is perfectly permissible for a state statute to limit powers of attorney to persons related by blood or marriage.[3] A state may also mandate separate documents for financial and medical decisions, or require specific formalities such as witnesses or notaries. There are several books directed at lesbian and gay men that discuss durable powers of attorney, including providing advice and forms.[4] Additionally, many state statutes themselves provide forms within the text of the statutes.

Powers of attorney are valuable tools with possible practical effects for the daily survival of lesbians. That any desired practical effects are only possibilities—and not certainties—is important to remember. As is the case with wills leaving property at one's death, powers of attorney are also subject to legal challenges by disgruntled family members. There are many legal theories that support such challenges, including the popular claim that one lover has exerted "undue influence" or fraud upon the other.

Thus, while the existence of a durable power of attorney might have prevented the Kowalski litigation, it is no guarantee as a preventative or even an outcome determinant. A lack of absolute certainty applies to legal documents, but for lesbians this lack of certainty is compounded. Nevertheless, durable powers of attorney (and similar documents like wills) are valuable tools that allow one to carve a niche in the legal edifice. They are not tools that can, in Audre Lorde's apt phrase, dismantle the master's house. But they are tools that can possibly improve the lot of those who are living (perhaps only temporarily) within the master's house. They are not always available, and not always foolproof, but they can override the laws honoring *family* that would otherwise operate.

Like all rules of law, I think that however practical the rules for durable powers of attorney may be, they should also be evaluated from a lesbian-centered perspective. From this point of view, powers of attorney and similar tools are generally unobjectionable. These tools are not confined to coupledom as conceptualized by the law; in fact, one might just as easily name a trusted friend to make one's medical decisions as a lover. Further, unless distorted, these tools have little impact upon the relationship. One may be flattered or impressed at being named as someone's "attorney," and a mutual naming may indicate commitment and trust, but the purpose of these tool-type documents is outer directed: they seek to prevent third parties from taking advantage of the rule of law that privileges nonlesbian relationships. The documents themselves do not give one person any rights vis-à-vis the other, and they do not define the relationship. When legal documents do give lesbians rights vis-à-vis each other and define the relationship, as is the case with relationship contracts, I believe they fall into a different category.

Contracts of Love

An amazing array of lesbian advisors who agree on little else agree that relationship contracts are great ideas. Lesbian advisors concerned with the law rightly point out that an explicit written agreement can prevent a lot of nasty arguing in a courtroom about who-promised-what-when. Lesbian advisors unconcerned with the law rightly point out that an explicit written agreement can prevent a lot of arguments in a household about who-promised-what-when. Yet despite their good points, I think relationship contracts exhibit a destructive potential to domesticate lesbian relationships.

Contracts, whether written or oral, state the obligations of, and benefits to, the parties to the contract. As such, a contract gives each person rights that are legally enforceable against the other person(s) to the contract, even if a party never intended such a result. There are numerous cases where courts have found written contracts, oral contracts, or implied contracts, despite one person's protests that a contract was never intended. Given this possibility, the most sensible choice might be to formally execute a written document that would be the relationship contract. Yet one must remember that such a relationship contract is a choice to resort to the rule of law, even if it is never litigated. The rule of law becomes a part of the relationship.

A contract is a legal creature, and by using a contract as an expression of a lesbian relationship, we define our relationship in the terms of legal ideology. We become domesticated when the rule of law is our lesbian "common sense," when we start to relate to each other as bargaining parties. Although Pat Califia has proposed that rather than issuing ultimatums, one should think of forming a relationship as the "process of negotiating a contract,"[5] the contract solution may not be any better than its alternative if lesbianism is about something other than bargaining to trade this-for-that. I'll love you if you love me. I'll do the dishes if you take out the garbage. Such agreements may seem ridiculous or fair, but when they are conceptualized as contractual arrangements, they rely upon the rule of law, and in particular, a rule of law meant to enforce the (free) market economy.[6] Do we really want to express our love, our commitment, or our daily tasks in the terms set by the rule of law? The difficulty we have in imagining anything different is attributable to our domestication. Contracting has become part of our common sense. In doing so, it forecloses the development of a lesbian sense that might be different.

When we participate in a relationship contract, we are participating in a very specific legal ideology. It is generally agreed that classical contract doctrine is derived from "original contracts" such as those between Man and the State. Critics of this classical contract doctrine point out that the contract legitimates privilege through the creation of neutral-sounding rights. The neutrality of these rights is supported by two basic contract myths: the myth that the contracting people have freely chosen to contract, and the myth that the contracting people are equal.[7]

Applied to lesbian relationship contracts, the myths that support contract ideology obscure realities of lesbian existence. First, it is too easy to assume that lesbians entering a relationship contract have freely chosen to do so. I have indulged in this assumption myself. But if freedom is more than not being coerced—as in the classic legal example of someone holding a gun to someone's head—this may not be true. If one thinks about the unanimity among lesbian advisors that relationship contracts are good, and perhaps the views of one's own lover, making a relationship contract can be more like acquiescence than free choice. Further, if we consider the primacy of and emphasis on relationship(s) in many lesbian cultures, combined with heterosexuality's tangible indications of the exhaltation of coupledom (weddings, marriage certificates), it is possible that neither our longing for a relationship nor for a tangible indication of our relationship are truly freely chosen. Contract theorists disputing the freedom of choice in employment contracts often argue eloquently that workers have little choice about the jobs they take, the wages they are paid, and the conditions under which they work, given a market economy. We might say the same of the relationship ethic.

Second, and I think more troubling, is contract ideology's assumption that the contracting parties are equal. This equality myth may never be more powerful than at the beginning stages of a relationship—the very time at which a relationship contract is advised—if we believe even half of what we've heard about the "merging" of lesbian couples. The contract assumption of equality obscures not only the differences that may develop during an extended relationship, but also the very real social, cultural, racial, economic, physical, and emotional differences among lesbians. For example, one might have a particular view of entering into a contract if one is an African-American lesbian whose own great-grandmother has been the object bargained for in a contract signed by slavers. And one might have a particular view if one is a lower-class lesbian who is unaccustomed to "asking" for things. In both of these examples there is a great deal of ambivalence that cannot simply be factored in an equation for contract equality. The African-American lesbian whose ancestors have been excluded from the right to contract may feel empowered by her ability to do so, as may the lower-class lesbian who feels that she is able to ask rather than forced to bargain.[8] Just as the Married Women's Property Acts in the nineteenth century empowered many women by allowing them to enter into contracts for the first time, so, too, can entering into a lesbian relationship contract empower lesbians, both on a practical survival level and on a political/personal level.

What all of these various advantages and disadvantages of relationship contracts suggest is that any absolute position is simplistic. The potential for domestication and the potential for concrete benefits and empowerment are both important considerations. Each lesbian must make the choice about relationship contracts for herself. In doing so, I think the following are useful considerations:

- an individual consideration of one's relationship to contracts (and perhaps legal documents in general) based upon personal and social histories;
- an individual or couple/group consideration of the myths of freedom and equality as they relate to this specific contract situation;
- an individual or couple/group consideration of the specific purposes of the contract, and in light of these purposes the specific contents of the relationship contract; and
- a couple/group discussion of the potential for the relationship contract to become a document enforced by law, whether or not either party wishes it to be so used.

The choice one makes is important, but I think it is more important that one makes her choice after considering the possibilities of domestication and concrete benefits/empowerment. The goal is to use the law's methodology without being used by it, to put contract in its place rather than assume positions within it.

State Approval

The marriage contract is the ultimate institution of coupledom. In this contract, the state sets the terms and conditions; the parties have relatively little freedom to bargain. The state also polices the borders of this contract by defining who can get in, as well as policing if and how people who are in can get out. For lesbians, the state's police power is relatively uniform. Lesbians cannot participate in the marriage contract with other lesbians. If a lesbian marries a man, his claim of her lesbianism may be enough to get an annulment—a judicial declaration that the marriage never existed.

At one time, many states enforced laws that prohibited "nonwhite" persons from marrying "white persons." Such miscegenation laws were declared unconstitutional by the United States Supreme Court in the relatively recent 1967 case of *Loving v. Virginia*, in which the Court reasoned, in part, that marriage was a fundamental right.[9] Those handful of lesbians and gay men who have litigated their right to marry have relied upon Loving to challenge laws that prohibit same-sex/gender marriages. The courts that have considered this claim have unanimously decided that laws limiting the state-created contract of marriage to pairs of opposite-sex couples are constitutionally valid.

Courts find no violation of equality doctrine because "homosexuals" are not a class entitled to heightened protection, and the state laws are rationally related—in legal terms—to the state's interest in regulating marriage. Litigants who raise the possibility of gender as well as sexual orientation discrimination are told that there is no gender discrimination because women cannot marry women and men cannot marry men; there would only be gender discrimination if men could marry men but women could not marry women (or vice versa). Courts also find no violation of the fundamental right to marriage because marriage is defined as one man and one woman, according to the courts' own "common sense."[10]

Given the passage of statutes and ordinances prohibiting sexual orientation discrimination (discussed in chapter 6), there have been several new—thus far unsuccessful—challenges to the limitation of marriage to heterosexual couples. Such lawsuits, however, as well as ordinances and statutory proposals for marriage or domestic partnership, raise the larger issue of lesbian marriage. The controversies surrounding the prospect of lesbian marriage illustrate the central preoccupation of *Lesbian (Out)law*—making choices about lesbian survival, both survival in our daily lives and as lesbians.

For those lesbians in coupled relationships, a state-sanctioned marriage could have numerous benefits contributing to lesbian survival. There are economic benefits including tax considerations, social security, workers compensation, health insurance coverage, and private employer benefits, as well as other benefits such as immigration preferences, and inclusion in housing regulations. Further, if a lesbian couple were legally married, there would be little need to provide for one's lover by using the tools discussed in the first part of this chapter because the operative laws would favor the lesbian "spouse." Specific benefits are the subject of litigation in various parts of the country. One of many examples is the suit by the Gay [and Lesbian] Teachers Association of New York City against the Board of Education seeking health insurance benefits for domestic partners on the same terms available to spouses.[11] Additionally, domestic partnership laws in a number of cities allow municipal workers and sometimes others to reap spousal benefits if they are registered with the government as domestic partners.

While there might be many practical disadvantages for a married lesbian couple depending on their circumstances, including increased tax liability, decreased financial aid including public assistance, and the costs of any divorce, the opposition to lesbian marriage by lesbians is mainly rooted in concerns about the less tangible aspects of lesbian survival. One aspect is lesbian solidarity and the perception that state-approved marriage divides lesbians. A class division is evident in observations that the benefits of lesbian marriage mainly accrue to lesbians of a certain class. At least one lesbian has to have a job with the type of employer who provides group health insurance benefits before such benefits become important. A sexual division is evident in observations that state-approved marriage draws lines between good lesbians and deviant ones. An acceptable lesbian is one who has a state-approved marriage and limits her lesbian sex to the marital bed.[12]

Another concern derives not from lesbian solidarity, but from lesbian identity as coinciding with gender identity. Historically, the state contract of marriage has been repressive to women. If contract ideology has its problems, marriage ideology is monstrous in comparison. There is a well-established rule of law that when a "man and wife" are married they become one person, and that person is the man. This rule of law has relaxed a great deal in recent years, but less than twenty years ago it was still being cited approvingly by courts.

I find the arguments against marriage convincing, even when they extend to quasi-marriage arrangements offered by the state, including domestic partnership. And I do not find convincing the argument that as lesbians we can enter the state-created marriage contract and transform it by our very participation. Perhaps I am not optimistic enough. Or perhaps I am too intimidated by articles with titles like "A Conservative Argument for Gay Marriage" that seek to welcome respectable gay men and lesbians into the family "since persecution is not an option in a civilized society."[13] Whatever the reason, I think that our participation in marriage and marriagelike arrangements domesticates our relationships. If making contracts has the potential to domesticate us in the direction of bargaining, marriage can lead to other forms of domestication. Our relationships become subject to enforced monogamy, for example, since the laws of most states make adultery a crime, or a suitable reason for divorce in states that require one. Whether or not we believe that monogamy is a good idea in our particular situation is not the question; rather, whether we are willing to allow the rule of law to make and enforce that decision for us. The terms of the marriage contract are often both common knowledge *and* obscure. What is always true, however, is that we do not have any control over them. They are subject to the rule of law, the specifics of which can be changed. While it might seem that the laws of marriage are ancient and constant, one need only think about women who married in the 1950s and became good (house)wives in accordance with the prevailing rules of law, only to be divorced in the 1980s and become poor in accordance with the new prevailing rules of law.

My own conclusion is that our quest for lesbian survival is not furthered by embracing the law's rule of marriage. Our legal energy is better directed at abolishing marriage as a state institution and *spouse* as a legal category.

This conclusion also applies to our arguments to be included within the legal category of *family*. While the "family of affinity" recognized by the Minnesota appellate court in the Kowalski case contributes to a good result, its reasoning is not necessarily cause for acclaim. The legal category of *family* is a bit more diffuse than the legal category of *spouse*, but ultimately it may be just as domesticating.

REFERENCES

Ruthann Robson and S.E. Valentine, *Lov(h)ers: Lesbians as Intimate Partners and Lesbian Legal Theory*, 63 TEMPLE LAW REVIEW 511 (1990).

ENDNOTES

1. The information and quotes are derived from KAREN THOMPSON AND JULIE ANDRZEJEWSKI, WHY CAN'T SHARON KOWALSKI COME HOME? (San Francisco, California: Spinsters/Aunt Lute 1988).

2. _____ N.W.2d _____ (Minn. App. 1991).

3. See, e.g., Florida Statute §709.08.

4. For example, see H. CURRY AND D. CLIFFORD, A LEGAL GUIDE FOR LESBIAN AND GAY COUPLES (5th ed. 1989). For another example aimed at attorneys, see NATIONAL LAWYERS GUILD, SEXUAL ORIENTATION AND THE LAW (ed. Roberta Achtenberg 1989).

5. PAT CALIFIA, SAPPHISTRY 57 (Tallahassee, Florida: Naiad Press 1980).

6. Thus, contract is similar to what lesbian ethicist Sarah Hoagland calls the "mercantile culture" in her book LESBIAN ETHICS (Palo Alto, California: Institute for Lesbian Studies 1989), see esp. at 274.

7. For a feminist discussion of contract, see CAROLE PATEMAN, THE SEXUAL CONTRACT (1988).

8. The example relating to African-American responses to contract is derived from the work of Patricia Williams, recently gathered together in her book THE ALCHEMY OF RACE AND RIGHTS (1991). The example relating to lower-class responses to contract is derived from my own experiences, and from specific pieces by Chrystos, *Headaches and Ruminations,* 17 GAY COMMUNITY NEWS 9, February 4-10, 1990, and Cartyis Cardea, *Lesbian Revolution and the Fifty Minute Hour,* in LESBIAN PHILOSOPHIES AND CULTURES (Jeffner Allen ed. 1990).

9. Loving v. Virginia, 388 U.S. 1 (1967).

10. See generally, Baker v. Nelson, 291 Minn. 310, 191 N.W.2d 185 (1971), appeal dismissed, 409 U.S. 810 (1972); Singer v. Hara, 11 Wash. App. 247, 522 P.2d 1187 (1974).

11. The teachers rely not only on constitutional theories, but on local and state laws, especially the Governor's Executive Order prohibiting discrimination on the basis of sexual orientation.

12. This view is articulated by lesbian attorney Paula Ettlebrick in many speeches and is printed as *Since When Is Marriage a Path to Liberation?,* 6 OUT/LOOK 9 (1989). The contrary view is articulated by her then coworker at the Lambda Legal Defense and Education Fund, Tom Stoddard, in the same publication.

Of course, legalized lesbian marriage would not invent the good lesbian/deviant lesbian dichotomy. As Joan Nestle argues, lesbian purity in the "cloak of monogamous long term relationships" is an image that we accept at our own peril. JOAN NESTLE, A RESTRICTED COUNTRY 123 (Ithaca, New York: Firebrand Books 1987).

13. Andrew Sullivan, *The Case for Gay Marriage,* THE NEW REPUBLIC (August 28, 1989). The issue's cover featured two white men in tuxedos holding hands on a wedding cake.

11

LESBIANS WITH CHILDREN

ike legal categories defining relationships between adult lesbians, legal categories defining relationships between lesbians
and children pose problems. The legal category that dominates
lesbian relationships with children is that of *mother*. While mother is
certainly a category that is not only legal, its importance as a legal category must not be underestimated. The extent to which a lesbian is
a legally recognized mother is the extent to which a lesbian's relationship with a child might be protected. Yet even if this relationship is
legally defined as mother-child, this does not guarantee absolute protection. The law may determine that a particular lesbian is not within
the category of mother as the law defines it. In such a case, the law
denies the lesbian custody or visitation and places the child with another person or with the state.

Unlike many of the other subjects discussed in *Lesbian (Out)-
law,* the subject of lesbian custody has received considerable legal attention.[1] Much of this attention has been by legal reformers and scholars who are responsible for many of the changes in the rule of law
that benefit lesbians who seek to maintain relationships with children.
It must be stressed at the outset, however, that any lesbian legal theory cannot assume that lesbian custody is the preferable outcome. As
always, the emphasis must be on lesbian choice.

Lesbian Mothers and Nonlesbian Challenges

Lesbians relationships with children are subject to legal interference by two general categories of nonlesbians. (Disputes between lesbians are considered in the next section). The first category is the other parent, the father. The relationship between mother-child-father is a legal one. For lesbians who share parentage of a child with a man, regardless of whether they have been married to the man, or engaged in heterosexual intimacies with the man, or perhaps even used the man's donated sperm, the law dictates that the man has parental rights. The rules of law determining men's parental rights have fluctuated throughout legal history. At one time the father had an absolute right to sole custody (of legitimate children), an obvious result given the man's ownership of both the wife and the children. The more recent American rules of law generally employed a maternal preference, especially if the child was of "tender years." This so-called tender years doctrine gave the mother a presumption of custody unless the father could prove the mother was unfit. Under this standard, many lesbians were, in fact, so judged. The tender years doctrine did not change because of lesbian legal reform, however, but because of the relatively recent feminist legal reform that led to the establishment of gender-neutral laws. Thus, the present rule of law in all states provides that in custody litigations between the mother and father, the court must determine the "best interests of the child." This gender-neutral rule supposedly allows the parents to start off in equal positions. The court then applies numerous factors depending upon the particular state statute or case law in order to weigh the relative merits of the parents. Factors considered include economic, educational, social, and cultural ones, and given women's disadvantage in these areas relative to men, it is not unexpected to learn from current statistics that fathers who litigate for custody have a substantial chance of prevailing. Also not surprisingly, the best-interests-of-the-child test often is applied as if it is the best-interest-of-the-state test, especially when judges reason that it is in the best interests of a child to grow up in a conventional state-approved family.

When lesbianism is raised in a case between a mother and a father, whether it is in an original custody case or in a suit seeking a change of custody because of the discovery of the mother's lesbianism, courts employ three different approaches. The first and most limiting approach is that living with a lesbian mother cannot be in the best interests of the child. The second or middle approach is that living with a lesbian mother can be in the best interests of a child as long

as the mother is a mother and not a lesbian who flaunts her lesbianism, lives with a lesbian lover, or engages in lesbian politics. The third
and presumably most enlightened approach is the nexus approach.
Courts use this test to determine whether the mother's lesbianism actually harms the child.

In practice, the application of this harm principle often makes
the nexus test indistinguishable from the first *per se* approach or the
middle ground mother-first lesbian-last approach. The types of harm
considered by the courts under this nexus test include the harm of
molestation (although this is more likely to be emphasized in a gay
father's case than a lesbian mother's); the harm of a potential gay or
lesbian identity in the child; the harm of stigmatization to the child
because of having a lesbian mother; and the harm of living in an immoral and illegal environment. For example, in a 1989 Missouri appellate court opinion, the court specifically adopted the requirement
that there must be "a nexus between harm to the child and the parent's homosexuality," but considered it evidence of harm that the
"mother admitted on cross-examination that she had slept with a
friend while the children were in the house. She was also unable to
'say for certain' that she had not kissed the friend on the lips or
touched her affectionately in front of the children." The court also
noted that even if the "mother remains discreet about her sexual
preference, a number of experts at the trial testified and Missouri case
law recognizes that a parent's homosexuality can never be kept secret
enough to be a neutral factor in the development of a child's values
and character."[2] The appellate court affirmed the trial court's award of
custody to the father, and his new wife, despite the fact that each child
told the trial judge that he or she wished to remain with the mother.
Not all courts have applied the nexus test, or even the middle ground
approach, as homophobically as the Missouri court. Many courts, including appellate courts in New Jersey, Alaska, Massachusetts, South
Carolina, and New York have specifically found that a mother's lesbianism did not constitute a harm to the child.[3] However, underlying
even these relatively liberal opinions filled with fact-specific reasoning is the assumption that having a lesbian mother could be harmful
to a child, and thus considered not to be in the best interests of the
child, that future citizen of the state.

Lesbian relationships with children are also subject to legal
interference by nonlesbians who are not parents to the child. These
third parties can include interested relatives, foster parents, or the state.
In these cases, the third party must generally prove the mother unfit. The rule of law does not impose equality upon the mother and the

nonparent, and these third parties have a higher burden than simply proving that it would be in the best interests of the child to remove the child from the lesbian mother. Courts do not generally consider lesbianism alone proof of unfitness, but this does not mean courts do not consider it, or even rely on it. For example, in a 1990 case from the Supreme Court of Mississippi, the court affirmed an award of custody to the paternal grandparents of the children of a lesbian mother, An-(drea) White. Mississippi's highest court noted that even though the trial court "may have relied almost exclusively" on the mother's lesbian relationship, there was enough evidence in the record—including some conflicting testimony about the children being outside in cold weather without adequate clothing—to support the trial court's removing the children from An White's custody, as well as not allowing the children to visit with her in the presence of her lover. The mother in this case is not a middle-class model of respectability, but what is interesting is that she was not that model when she was married; in fact, her conditions had apparently improved since she separated from her husband and began living with her lover. No one claimed that the children's father should be awarded custody "given his financial situation and his drinking problem." Yet when An White became involved with a woman, her husband's parents decided that she should be denied custody. The courts of Mississippi agreed.[4]

The *per se* rule of law that *lesbian* and *mother* are mutually exclusive legal categories is in disrepute. The enlightened view, subject to many permutations, is that lesbianism alone cannot satisfy the requirement of a mother being unfit should third parties attempt to gain custody, or even the requirement that custody be awarded to the parent who most judiciously comports with the best interests of the child should a father attempt to gain custody. This enlightened view has been forced upon the courts by many brave lesbian mothers who engaged in painful litigation with the advocacy of many hard-working and clever lesbian legal workers. It is certainly an advancement.

Nevertheless, this step in the right direction represents the patina of privilege. Like the idea of lesbian marriage, these liberal custody rules of law contribute to a division between bad lesbians and good ones, as well as dividing children similarly. Two examples are illustrative. First, there is Jane Doe, so good that she keeps her real name out of the court records. Jane does not have sole custody of her son, the eleven-year-old "well-adjusted and above-average" Jack, but he visits her eight weeks in the summer and alternate Easter and Christmas vacations. Ann Smith Doe, the father's new wife, wants to adopt Jack and thus terminate Jane Doe's parental rights. A Virginia trial court agrees, terminates Jane's status as a mother, and allows the adoption. But when Jane appeals to the Supreme Court of Virginia, she prevails. The court's opinion sounds like she is winning the contest for Miss Congeniality rather than a custody appeal:

> Although there was testimony that her relationship with the woman with whom she lives is unorthodox, the testimony is also that Jane Doe is an exceptionally well-educated, stable, responsible, and sensitive individual. Witnesses described Jane in various ways, but always in a highly complimentary manner. They referred to her as a conscientious and creative parent, friendly by nature, who instills in the boy a love for other people and for animals. It was testified that Jane's love for Jack was a nurturing love, and that she exercised a selfless wisdom in caring for him. Jane Doe has apparently earned the respect of her peers. . . because of her civic work and active interest in the community and her relationship with the people with whom she comes into contact.[5]

I do not mean to belittle Jane Doe, or the accomplishment of her attorney for putting together such impressive evidence, but factors such as being well-educated and engaging in civic work can be a bit daunting to someone like An White, who lived in a trailer and had most recently worked at a convenience store. Also daunting, in addition to the class considerations, are lesbian-identity issues. As the Supreme Court of Virginia specifically noted, it was not "approving, condoning, or sanctioning" Jane's "unnatural lifestyle" which was proper for the court to consider, but found that it was outweighed in her particular circumstances, a resolution which the court warned might be temporary: "Further, in determining her fitness as a mother and the future welfare of her son, we are not unmindful of her testimony that should it become necessary, for her son's sake, she would sever the relationship with the woman with whom she now lives. There may come a time when the welfare and best interest of her son require that she honor this commitment."

For women who are not willing to separate from their lesbian lovers, courts are less lenient. They are especially prone to less leniency if the mother in question is less than congenial, a little too dykey, and the child is less than perfect. In a Pennsylvania case, the mother appealed the state's taking away of her preschool son who had a speech problem. The appellate court upheld the removal, writing an opinion containing the following: "[J]oey was exposed to a chaotic and harmful home life. The mother is a lesbian who effects a masculine appearance, wears men's clothing, and has a masculine oriented mental status. At the time of the hearing, she lived with Nancy M. and two of her children in a two bedroom apartment. . . . [The caseworker] also found the mother to be uncooperative. The mother took notes throughout her meetings with the caseworker and responded in an adversarial manner that her attorney, J.D. 'knows about this. . . .' "[6]

When the mother refused the condition that she not live with her lover, the court found that this "revealed forcefully her true feelings and attitudes regarding Joey's [speech] therapy." The appellate court disingenuously rejected the mother's claim that the court was unnecessarily interfering in her lesbian relationship absent a causal connection between the lesbianism and harm. The court noted that the order to exclude the lover from their home was not meant to interfere with the lesbian relationship, only to establish order and foster the close relationship between the mother and son.

When conflicts over a child arise between a lesbian and a heterosexual man or state agency, our lesbian loyalties are undivided. Any lesbian legal theory must center the lesbian and privilege her position to choose custody. In most cases, a lesbian in a custody dispute has not chosen to be within the rules of law. There must be legal reform to afford lesbians who find themselves within that legal system their choices. A liberal nexus test that states that harm must be proven or else lesbianism will not be considered is not liberal enough; harm must not include a child being exposed to lesbian expression or a child's potential lesbianism or gayness. Exclusion of a lesbian's lover from her home is asking a lesbian to choose between her lover and her child. This is not the type of lesbian choice that any lesbian legal theory would seek to promote.

Yet a lesbian legal theory must stress lesbian choice rather than lesbian custody. An assumption that custody is what should be chosen by any lesbian is detrimental. A lesbian legal theory puts lesbians at the center, even to the exclusion of the children of lesbians. It is difficult to disagree with the legal standard of "best interests of the child," but a lesbian legal theory has a different focus. Its central focus is lesbian.

Lesbian Mothers and Gay/Lesbian Coparents

When conflicts over a child within our community arise, our lesbian loyalties can be divided: centering lesbians does not necessarily solve the problems arising from the separation of two lesbians who are raising a child together. Before considering this scenario, however, I think it should be distinguished from another one in which lesbian loyalties can be falsely divided and centering lesbians does reorient our perspective. The scenario involves the gay sperm donor.

Under the rule of law, contribution of sperm is an entitlement to the benefits and burdens of fatherhood. Many states do have statutes that alleviate this rule somewhat, but importantly, these statutes protect the rights of infertile fathers by severing the sperm donor's father-right when insemination is performed by a licensed physician on a married woman. This severing is consistent with the rule of law's limitation of parentage: a child has one father and one mother, no more and no less. In the case of a woman married to an infertile man, the rule of law declares that the husband is the child's father and not the sperm donor. In the case of an unmarried woman, there is no husband to assume the role of father. A court, ever eager to promote fatherhood, allows the donor the appellation *father* and awards him visitation.

Illustrative of this scenario is the California case of *Jhordan C. v. Mary K.* Although the court never tells us that Mary K. is a lesbian, the opinion does tell us that Mary decided to have a child by "artificial insemination" jointly with "Victoria, a close friend." After making that decision, "Mary sought a semen donor by talking with friends and acquaintances. This led to three or four potential donors with whom Mary spoke directly. She and Victoria ultimately chose Jhordan after he had one personal interview with Mary and one dinner at Mary's home." Without discussing Jhordan's sexuality, the court affirmed the award of Jhordan's visitation. The court also rejected Mary's constitutional challenges to the insemination statute, raised on her behalf by her attorney, Roberta Achtenberg of the Lesbian Rights Project.[7]

The result in Mary's case is troubling. While the court did not award Jhordan the joint custody he sought (which would have allowed him to participate in day-to-day decisions about the child), it did grant him father-status and generous visitation. However, what I find more troubling is a shift in lesbian legal strategies since the mid-1980s when *Mary K.* came before a California appellate court. In the past year, I have heard of numerous cases of gay men who have been sperm donors now seeking court-ordered visitation of three, four, ten, and thirteen-year-old children. The lesbians defending these actions have often been denied representation and support from the organized gay/lesbian legal community. The gay/lesbian legal reform agenda is devoted to an expansion of the legal concept of family, including visitation for gay men who have been sperm donors and now decide to establish father-right. With the rule of law in their favor, gay men who have been sperm donors can most often win an award of visitation. It does not matter whether visitation is desired by the lesbians who have been caring for the child since birth. And it matters little whether visitation is desired by the child, for courts will presume and court-ordered psychologists will declare that a child should have contact with a "father."

If we center lesbians rather than gay/lesbian concerns, this controversy demands a different result. The rights of men, whether gay or not, are not the focus of any lesbian legal theory. Just as marriage has a legal history of dominance of men over women, so, too, does father-right. What needs to be preserved is lesbian choice, not father-right.

Likewise, if we center lesbians rather than law—even law as expressed by the lesbian/gay legal reform movement—our loyalties are undivided. Again, what we must preserve is lesbian choice, not the legal category *family*, however alternative or expansive.

The centering of lesbians is more difficult when the dispute is between two lesbians. In a situation in which two lesbians have a baby, the biological mother is the legal mother. The other lesbian is profoundly "other": she is a legal stranger to her child, just as she is a legal stranger to her lover. As in the case of lovers when no child is involved, centering lesbians requires a distinction between situations involving third parties and those between lesbians. In third-party situations, legal tools may prevent the operation of laws that privilege the legal category family in the event one of the lesbians dies or becomes incapacitated. The death or incapacitation of the biological/legal mother can interfere with the relationship between the "other" mother and the child. The biological mother can express her desires in a will or other document, but although the law at times regards children almost akin to property, in fact they are not property and cannot be willed. However, a court can take into account the biological mother's statement in the event of a custody dispute, and there is no apparent negative to such a statement. A medical guardianship is a document that can allow an adult to make medical decisions for a child. Like the wills and powers of attorney discussed in the previous chapter, these documents are outer-directed and not intended to give the lesbians rights vis-à-vis each other. Again, as in relationships without children, many suggest the solution of contracts. A contract cannot have as its subject the child (this would be baby-selling and considered illegal), but a contract could give the adults rights against each other. However, the contract solution suffers the same problems in this context as in a childless context. The danger is that lesbians adopt the assumptions of contract, and that particular lesbians may be disempowered by the operation of those assumptions.

The most often-posed legal solution has been adoption, a recognized legal procedure that allows a nonbiological parent to become a legal parent. Until very recently, however, courts have been unanimous in their conclusion that parents are limited to being either a mother or a father: a child cannot have two mothers by adoption or otherwise; and a female parent must be a mother. Lesbian legal reformers have argued this point, in both impressive scholarship and in the courts. A 1991 District of Columbia opinion is apparently the first to allow one lesbian to adopt the child born to her lover. The court was troubled by the statute that provided that an adoption terminated the rights of the biological mother. The court, however, decided that the statute's language was only directive; the biological mother's rights did not have to be terminated.[8] In this same case, the court also allowed a previously adopted child to be adopted by the other lesbian parent as well, and there have been a few cases of two lesbians simultaneously adopting one child.

Absent an adoption, there are legal theories that might support a lesbian parent being awarded custody of a child should the biological parent die or become incapacitated. Such theories include de facto parenthood (also called psychological parenthood), equitable parenthood, and in loco parentis. In each of these theories, the adult's actions that emulate parenthood are adjudicated by a court to determine whether or not the adult will be legally deemed a parent. The actions are judged not only against an ideal parent's, but also against any other parentlike adults in the child's life. At times, formal legal rights would be in direct conflict with these creative theories. Should a biological mother die, for example, custody of the child might be awarded on the basis of the recognized father status of a sperm donor rather than the less formal psychological parent status of the lesbian parent. If the parents of the deceased lesbian seek custody of the child from the surviving lesbian parent, their grandparent status is entitled to some weight, but is less compelling than father status.[9]

All of these theories, including adoption, can be used like tools to forestall the effect of the rules of law that would otherwise operate. I think they can be useful in that capacity. Using these tools in a prospective way as much as possible is also good practical advice. Thus, to the extent that any tool can dissuade third parties from seeking custody of a child, the more useful the tool. When these theories are the basis of a contest between lesbians waged in the legal arena, however, we turn the tools and rules of law upon each other.

If two lesbians decide to have a child together, do so, and then decide to separate, the child's future becomes uncertain. In the best of all possible lesbian utopias, the two lesbians would exercise their lesbian choices in a way that honored themselves, each other, and the child. There would be no need to resort to the rules of law. But one lesbian can decide that she is the true and only mother, and if she is the biological mother (and there is no adoption), the rule of law will enforce her decision. And the other lesbian can sue her ex-lover for visitation with the child, utilizing theories to persuade the court that she should be accorded at least some parental rights. She will be represented by gay/lesbian legal reform organizations, arguing for recognition of the lesbian family as analogous to the nuclear family. Other gay/lesbian rights organizations will file briefs as interested parties urging the court to expand the legal category of *family* to include both lesbian parents (and perhaps even the gay male sperm donor). In the courts that have considered this scenario, the nonbiological lesbian parent will lose. Despite the courts' opinions, there is a groundswell of liberal popular support for expanding legal concepts of parenthood and family to include the nonbiological lesbian parent.

The case of *Alison D. v. Virginia M.* is an example. Decided in 1991 by New York's highest court, the decision rejects a claim for visitation from a lesbian nonbiological mother, concluding that she is not a parent within the meaning of the statute. Represented by Paula Ettlebrick of Lambda Legal Defense and Education Fund, and supported by briefs from the NOW Legal Defense Fund, the ACLU, and the Gay and Lesbian Parents Coalition, Alison D. argued that she was a de facto parent entitled to visitation. Although the same court had the year before given an expansive reading to the term *family* in a rent stabilization case involving a surviving male lover, the court here declined to give a similar expansive reading to the term *parent*. Judge Judith Kaye, the only judge on New York's highest court who could even remotely be called a feminist, was the only dissenting judge.[10]

Judge Kaye's dissent, and many reactions to the case from heterosexual feminists and liberal nonlesbians, are telling. Although a few feminists worried about the consequences for violence should de facto parent visitation include an abusive boyfriend of a battered woman, most sought to bring lesbians within preestablished legal definitions. Liberals extended their sympathies that lesbians were once again excluded.

Because Alison D. and Virginia M. are in conflict, it is difficult to center the concerns of both lesbians and not be inconsistent.

Yet this inconsistency—and the dispute itself—is constructed by the rule of law. To the extent that the biological mother Virginia M. supported her denial of visitation to her ex-lover with her superior position within the rules of law, she is domesticated by the legal regime. And to the extent that the nonbiological mother Alison D. believes she is entitled to visitation because she can fit herself into legal theories like in loco parentis, she is equally domesticated. When both lesbians appeal to the legalism inherent in categories like *parent* and *family* as they attempt to settle their problem, they import the law into their lesbianism, limiting themselves and all of us.

Thus, I am less concerned with the legal positions of Alison D. and Virginia M. than with how they came to make their claims in courts of law. This is not squeamishness about the public revelation of lesbians disagreeing, but concern that we are being used by the law rather than using it. My anxiety is the same whether Alison D. wins or loses; it is even more pronounced if Virginia M. merely appeals to her superior legal status to resolve disagreements with the woman she once loved.

Just as we must decide whether or not marriage is a legal category within which we can feel comfortable, so, too, must we make a parallel assessment about the legal category of *parent*. In the same way I do not find convincing the argument that as lesbians we can enter the state-created marriage contract and transform it by our very existence, I do not think that as lesbians (either singly or in pairs) we can enter the state-defined parent role and transform it. Again, perhaps I am not optimistic enough. Or perhaps I am too intimidated by the rules of law that operate in the parent-child relationship to give parents virtual ownership over their children unless the parents are not model state citizens. I am intimidated by the class and antilesbian model of the well educated and well-liked Jane Doe and her summers with her well-adjusted and above-average son. And I am intimidated by judicial disapproval profound enough to take a child away if a mother does not dress her children correctly in the Mississippi cold or does not dress herself correctly in feminine attire. Even absent a lesbian mother, the legal category of *mother* operates restrictively and punitively. Like the legal category of *marriage*, the legal category of *mother*, or *parent*, or even *family* is too stifling for our lesbian imaginations and relationships.

Domestication

Any lesbian legal theory must confront the legal domestication of our lesbianism. Litigation debates the terms and conditions of legal categories but rarely attacks the categories themselves. We need to challenge the categories if we are to insure lesbian survival, both on an individual and a group basis.

Like all the lesbians I know, my own experiences and ideas of motherhood/parenting are informed by categories other than the legal. I think that we cannot forget those other influences. I have often wondered whether my perceptions of legal domestication are profound because I have been educated, practicing, and teaching in the law for more than thirteen years. Yet my experiences of law as a domesticating force with regard to motherhood are often the result of hearing nonlegal workers appeal to the rules of law in nonlegal situations.

At the National Lesbian Conference in Atlanta last year, I participated in a workshop discussing lesbian parenting. None of the participants knew each other, and no one knew I was an attorney. During a small-group discussion, lesbians—ever practical—began talking about what our children should call us. My suggestion was that a child call both mothers simply by their first names. This suggestion was vigorously objected to by another lesbian who said, "The law gives me twenty-four-hours-a-day responsibility for that child. Me—and me only, not my lover and not anyone else. I deserve to be called something special, something that no one else calls me. Something like mother." What surprised me was not this lesbian's disagreement with my particular proposal, but her appeal to the law. Where I expected the birth pangs of biology, I got the legal rule of parental responsibility. The other members of the small group took up her point, agreeing not only with the special nature of the word *mother*, but appealing to its legal force.

When we talk about legal rules as the basis for lesbian choices, I believe we are domesticated. At stake is not whether the children who live with us call us Cindy or Mama Cindy or Mom. The range of choices is as wide as the range of lesbians. What is at stake is how we make such decisions. We can appeal to equality models in which no mother would be "other," antihierarchical models in which children are not deferential to adults, historical models in which children are property, and even personal models based upon our own childhoods. Or we can simply like the way something sounds. But when the reasoning for our lesbian decisions is predicated upon an uncritical adoption of the rule of law, we abdicate our lesbianism in favor of legalism.

This abdication also occurs in our thinking about problems other than naming ourselves. Whether or not two lesbians will choose litigation or other legal recourse against each other is a painful and often debilitating decision. Judgments about using the legal system in these instances are difficult. Yet filing a lawsuit is only the most obvious appeal to the rule of law. It is the less obvious—and more insidious—appeals that are potentially more harmful to lesbian survival.

ENDNOTES

1. Among the many fine pieces of legal scholarship on lesbian motherhood issues, the following are especially noteworthy: Nancy Polikoff, *This Child Does Have Two Mothers: Redefining Parenthood to Meet the Needs of Children in Lesbian-Mother and Other Nontraditional Families*, 78 GEORGETOWN LAW JOURNAL 459 (1990); Carmel Sella, *When A Mother Is a Legal Stranger to Her Child: The Law's Challenge to the Lesbian Nonbiological Mother*, 1 UCLA WOMEN'S LAW REVIEW 135 (1991); Annamay T. Sheppard, *Lesbian Mothers II: Long Night's Journey Into Day*, 8 WOMEN'S RIGHTS LAW REPORTER 219 (1985); Comment (by David S. Dooley), *Immoral Because They're Bad, Bad Because They're Wrong: Sexual Orientation and Presumptions of Parental Unfitness in Custody Disputes*, 26 CALIFORNIA WESTERN LAW REVIEW 395 (1990). Also especially noteworthy is an anthology of lesbian parenting issues: Sandra Pollack and Jeanne Vaughn, editors, POLITICS OF THE HEART (Ithaca, New York: Firebrand Books 1987).

2. T.C.H. v. K.M.H., 784 S.W.2d 281, 284-5 (Mo. Ct. App. 1989).

3. S.N.E. v. R.L.B., 699 P.2d 875 (Alaska 1985); Doe v. Doe, 452 N.E.2d 293 (Ma. 1983); M.P. v. S.P., 404 A.2d 1256 (N.J. 1979); Guinan v. Guinan, 102 A.D.2d 963, 477 N.Y.S.2d 830 (3rd Dept 1984); Stronman v. Williams, 353 S.E.2d 704 (S.C. 1987).

4. White v. Thompson, 569 So. 2d 1181 (Miss. 1990).

5. Doe v. Doe, 284 S.E.2d 799 (Va. 1981).

6. In re Breisch, 434 A.2d 815 (Pa. Super. Ct. 1981).

7. 179 Cal. App.3d 386, 224 Cal. Rptr. 530 (1st Dist. 1986).

8. In re Adoption of Minor T., D.C. Super Ct Fam. Div. Nos. A-269-90 & A-270-90 (August 30, 1991).

9. See e.g., In Re Pearlman, Florida Circuit Court Broward County, No. 87-24926 (March 31, 1989) 15 FAMILY LAW REPORTER 1355 (1989).

10. 77 N.Y.2d 651, 572 N.E.2d 27, 569 N.Y.S.2d 586 (1991).

LESBIANS AND VIOLENCE

12

THE VIOLENCE AGAINST US

Most of us do not need statistics to tell us about the violence against us. We have lived our lives as targets for hurled bottles, beery spit, and even bullets; we have been taunted by jeers, incessant threats of rape, and whispers. The violence against us is so pervasive as to be unremarkable. We live in it as the proverbial fish in water.

There has been an increasing awareness, in the last few years, about the violence against lesbians, as well as gay men and bisexuals, and a linking of this violence with the violence perpetrated on the basis of other group identities, such as race, ethnicity, religion, culture, and gender. Much of this awareness is due to the efforts of the Anti-Violence Project of the National Gay & Lesbian Task Force. Along with independent researchers and other antiviolence projects throughout the United States, the Anti-Violence Project has been documenting incidents of violence since the early 1980s.[1] According to their 1990 report, there were 1,588 incidents of anti-gay/lesbian violence in the United States that year. The report does not distinguish between lesbians and gay men, although some other surveys do. The social science wisdom concerning violence against lesbians consists of comparisons with the violence against gay men: we are much less likely to report the violence against us (one survey concludes that 91 percent of lesbians do not report the violence to any community agency); we are more likely than gay men to experience the violence from family members; and we are more likely to be sexually assaulted.

The rule of law has also begun to document the violence against us. Connecticut became the first state, in 1987, to pass a hate crimes statistics act, although this act contained only the vaguest definitions. In 1990, Congress passed the federal Hate Crime Statistics Act, which provides for the compilation of statistics of hate or bias crimes, specifically defined as "crimes that manifest evidence of prejudice based upon race, religion, sexual orientation, or ethnicity." The inclusion of sexual orientation as a category was the result of intense lobbying by lesbian and gay activists amidst much congressional controversy. The compromise necessary in Congress to preserve the sexual orientation category included a statement in the act that "the American family is the foundation of American society; federal policy should encourage the well-being, financial security, and health of the American family; and schools should not de-emphasize the critical value of American family life." Any doubts about the function of this paean to the family operating as an antidote to the mention of sexual orientation is resolved by the statute's next section: "Nothing in this Act shall be construed, nor shall any funds appropriated to carry out the purpose of the Act be used, to promote or encourage homosexuality." The federal act also includes an antidote to any possible judicial interpretation that a law requiring the collection of statistics about the violence against us might mean that discrimination against us is disfavored: "Nothing in this section creates a right to bring an action, including an action based on discrimination due to sexual orientation."[2]

Perhaps ironically, the very act which seeks to collect statistics about the violence against us is itself a manifestation of that violence. Many legal reformers believe that the repeal of statutes criminalizing lesbian sex and the passage of statutes protecting lesbians from discrimination are necessary steps in the quest to end violence against lesbians, but the act specifically rejects these goals. The signing of the Hate Crime Statistics Act marked the first time openly gay men and lesbians were invited to the White House. Yet under the very rule of law they have been invited to celebrate, lesbians cannot be promoted or encouraged or have any remedies against discrimination. Such ironies do not negate the federal act as an advancement, but do indicate the violence against us that inheres even in rules of law that implicitly disapprove of the violence against us.

The federal act also manifests violence against us through at least three strategies of categorization of our identities. First, the category *sexual orientation* is defined in the act as "consensual homosexuality and heterosexuality." Perhaps "consensual" is meant to modify both homosexuality and heterosexuality, but even assuming such a charitable interpretation, the very inclusion of heterosexuality is problematic. As in discrimination discourse, the category operates to obscure power differentials between heterosexuals and lesbians or gay men. For example, if a heterosexual man enters a lesbian bar and makes explicit heterosexual advances to the lesbian customers, and the lesbians shove him into the bathroom and lock him in there because they find such flagrant heterosexuality inappropriate and offensive, the lesbians have committed a hate crime, manifesting "evidence of prejudice" based on the sexual orientation of heterosexuality.

Second, the omission of the category *gender* from the federal act artificially isolates lesbianism. If a man rapes a lesbian and says, "What you need is a good fuck, dyke," the word *dyke* may be evidence of a hate crime. However, if the man rapes the same lesbian and neglects to say the word *dyke*, or says other words as well, or there are no other factors indicating his prejudice against lesbians, it might not be a hate crime. Not only is her lesbianism irrelevant, but rape itself is not a crime that "manifests evidence of prejudice" based on any category that the act recognizes.

Third, and most insidiously, the insistence on categorization itself violently atomizes us into separate identities. A rape of a lesbian, to use this example again, is not necessarily separable into discrete identities. As quoted in a recent article: "As I was being raped, I was called a dyke and a cunt. The rapist used those terms as if they were interchangeable. And as I talk to other women who have been raped—straight and gay—I hear similar stories. Was my attack antilesbian? Or was it antiwoman? I think the facts are simple. I was raped because as a woman I'm considered rapeable and, as a lesbian, I'm considered a threat. How can you separate those two things?"[3] Given the federal act, to count as a hate crime, the lesbian must stress her identity as a lesbian over her identity as a woman and hope that the FBI statisticians agree with her. A similar choice of categories occurs if the lesbian has other identities implicated in the crime but not included in the act, such as those based on old age or disability. To be counted, the lesbian must discount these identities if the relevant statute discounts them.

However, even when the lesbian has other identities implicated in the crime, and such identities are included in the act, choices of categories occur. Thus, in state statutes that include gender, the gender/sexuality dichotomy is not dissolved but has different consequences. These consequences are the same for all identities that are categories under a statistics act. For example, if under the federal act the rapist also makes racial slurs, such "evidence of prejudice" should mandate the statistic as a hate crime based on race. But a single incident is supposedly only to be reported once. Does the FBI statistician choose race or sexual orientation? Does the statistician ask the African-American lesbian whether she thinks she was raped because she is African-American or because she is a lesbian? Does the statistician ask the rapist? Any choice does violence to our experiences of the violence against us.

Perhaps paradoxically, however, the absence of categorization in a hate crime statistics act may be a fourth kind of violence. Just as the lack of sexual orientation in a state statute is a violent denial of the violence against us, and the lack of gender in the federal act is a violent denial of our experiences of the violence against us, and the insistence on categorization violently atomizes us into separate identities, the lack of any categories constitutes violence. Many opponents of hate crime bills seek to delete references to specific groups, usually lesbians and gay men. Failing that, another tactic is to seek to delete mention of any group identity. A hate crime act that mandates the collection of statistics of any crime based on bias, bigotry, or hate may appear to be magnanimously broad, but it actually erases the realities of violence. It also gives government officials wide latitude to determine the contours of bias, bigotry, and hate—allowing for the possibility that violence against lesbians is not biased, bigoted, or hateful—merely natural.

The power of the government official is also exercised in the determination of what counts as a hate crime, regardless of the category. A crime becomes a hate crime when government bureaucrats decide that it should be. The government workers making such determinations include police officers. Police departments are increasingly training officers to make final determinations about whether a suspected bias incident can be confirmed as such. For example, the New York City Police Department's Bias Incident Investigation Unit has issued guidelines stressing the officer's "common sense" in confirming bias incidents. The guidelines list considerations such as motive, display of offensive symbols, suspects' statements, victims' perceptions, and similarity to previous incidents. The guidelines even note that borderline cases should be resolved in favor of confirmation, although they also warn that "mere mention of a bias remark does not necessarily make an incident bias motivated," again stressing the use of common sense judgment. Given the historic hostility of law enforcement officials to lesbians—and the continuing evidence that the perpetrators of violence against us are quite likely to be police officers—it is not only the more cynical among us who find trusting the common sense of police officers to recognize the violence against us a bit ludicrous.

Critiques of the federal act mandating the collection of statistics often operate on the symbolic level because the act itself operates on this level. As a rule of law, the act is neither rule nor law. It provides no rights, no remedies, no penalties. It only requires the Attorney General to "acquire data" from 1990 until 1995 about crimes that manifest evidence of prejudice. Many believe that symbolism is insufficient to deter the violence against us.

The larger question is whether any rule of law can deter this violence. Those who find symbolism and statistics insufficient often advocate enhancement of penalties or more rigorous enforcement of criminal laws. Yet even these rules of law rely upon the formulation of a relatively new term, *hate crime*—its two parts in tension with each other. On the one hand, hate is usually not against any rule of law. On the other hand, a crime is a crime regardless of hate. This tension permeates the responses of the rule of law to the violence against us, resulting in two different perspectives: the special and the neutral.

The special model proposes that some crimes are worse than others and should be accorded special recognition. This is the model that looms behind the federal statistics act, allowing for special treatment in the statistical compilation of crimes evidencing hate. The enhancement of penalties proposal is also within this model. Penalty enhancement can be implemented by a statute that allows a judge to impose longer prison sentences on a finding that the crime was motivated by prejudice. For example, the New Hampshire enhancement statute, allowing judges to impose longer sentences in circumstances including prior convictions, was recently amended to include a hate crime provision: an extended term of imprisonment may be imposed if the defendant "was substantially motivated to commit the crime because of hostility toward the victim's religion, race, creed, sexual orientation, national origin, or sex."[4]

The neutral model suggests that existing criminal laws need to be enforced impartially. This model exhorts the rigorous enforcement of criminal laws and penalties, no matter that the victim is a lesbian. It is a principle advanced by lesbian and gay legal reformers protesting against judges who impose lenient sentences, or prosecutors who refuse to prosecute crimes committed against lesbians or gay men. A neutral principle is important any time a perpetrator raises a defense based upon the unimportance of the victim. While in practice, most of us recognize that the neutral principle is farcical given power differentials, we may nevertheless believe that if it were reality, the violence against us would be deterred. According to this perspective, what is needed is not special protection but equal treatment. And rigorous law enforcement.

The special approach and neutral approach often conflict in legal theory.[5] However, if we put lesbians at the center—rather than legal theory and its demands for consistency—perhaps this conflict is not troubling. Such a perspective would allow us to avail ourselves of whatever strategies the rules of law offer in order to deter the violence against us. Symbolism, statistics, enhancement, and enforcement—whatever is possible in our particular political situations.

Yet, by putting lesbians at the center, problems other than inconsistencies within legal theory become important. Many of the lesbians at the center experience the rule of law, particularly the criminal justice system, as racist, classist, and elitist. This experience impacts upon any strategies that implicate the criminal justice system, notwithstanding the empirical data that the perpetrators of the violence against us are most likely to be young white men from relatively privileged backgrounds. Even if we can put such considerations aside, or isolate our lesbian identities from all our other identities, the rule of law manifests its own violence against us. This violence makes it difficult to have confidence in the rule of law's interest in our lesbian survival.

The violence of the rule of law may seem to fade when we compare it to the violence against us that we endure daily. This daily violence is magnified and crystalized in the murder of Rebecca Wight and attempted murder of Claudia Brenner. The horror of it has been heard or read by most lesbians; its threatening possibility exists for each of us. The two lovers were camping on the Appalachian Trail in the spring of 1988 when they were assaulted by a barrage of bullets from a man who reportedly lived in a cave and had stalked them on the trail. The man, Stephen Roy Carr, was apprehended and charged with murder. The trial judge rejected his defense that he was provoked to murder them because he witnessed their lesbian lovemaking, and refused to hear evidence about his rejection by women and his mother's lesbianism. The judge convicted him of first degree murder and sentenced him to life imprisonment. Although he appealed, the appellate court agreed with the trial judge: "The sight of naked women engaged in lesbian lovemaking is not adequate provocation to reduce an unlawful killing from murder to voluntary manslaughter."[6] We can claim victory; justice was served.

Yet the jailing of Carr does not breathe life into any lesbian; it is the rule of law that is vindicated and not our lesbian existence. The rule of law punishes Carr, using a neutral approach that the victims did not deserve to be attacked. What remains unaddressed is the defendant's outsider status as an uncivilized "mountain man" that overrides the victims' outsider status as lesbians. What remains unaddressed are the social conditions that produce Carr's violence, although the rule of law encourages us to believe that the underlying violence has been addressed. A less well-known case is that of a New Hampshire man who confessed to the murder of two lesbians, after threatening them many times, because he said he "loathed their lifestyle." The man was prosecuted unsuccessfully three times and is now free. We cannot claim victory; justice was not served.

Yet one man's freedom does not mean that the lesbians are more dead: it is the rule of law that is implicated, not our lesbian existence. The rights of criminal defendants and the "loopholes" in the law, the trials, the lawyers, the judges, and the juries become the focus.

The rule of law encourages us to believe that it can redress and deter the violence against us, and in believing this, we are domesticated. But even when the perpetrator is quickly apprehended, convicted, and sentenced, the violence against us is not redressed or deterred. We find it almost impossible to think about other methods of redress or deterrence because we have so internalized the methodologies of the rules of law. The criminal justice system operates as therapeutic, and the critiques of therapy that are surfacing within lesbian theory are relevant. The prosecution solution is therapeutic in the sense that it is individualized and based more on our feelings about reality than our realities.

For lesbians who survive violence and enter the labyrinth of the criminal justice system as victims, the therapeutic effect of the rules of law can perpetuate the attack rather than redress it. The lesbian victims become part of a system over which they have no control; the prosecutor's career and the judge's calendar are the paramount considerations. Victims face the antilesbian attitudes of court system personnel. They face the possibility of accusations that they provoked the attack. Lesbians who are closeted face the public revelation of an identity that can be lawfully penalized in a variety of ways. This so-called secondary victimization can be as violent as the initial violence.[7] It domesticates us by absorbing our challenge to the violence against us into its own perpetuation of that violence. Even seemingly nonviolent responses within the rule of law can be domesticating. We are domesticated when we channel our fury at being attacked into a call to the FBI hotline. We are domesticated when we are grateful for an understanding officer from the bias task force unit. We are domesticated whenever we allow our own rage about the violence against us to be funneled into a belief that the rule of law will take care of everything.

For lesbians who survive violence and choose not to enter the labyrinth of the criminal justice system—statistically about 90 percent of us—the rule of law is also domesticating. I have even heard advocates within our own communities insist that each of us has a responsibility to report the violence against us to the police and agitate for prosecutions. For lesbians who do not follow this advice, domestication can take the form of guilt and an assumption of personal responsibility for the violence we have suffered. The (false) promise that the rule of law will remedy the violence against us if only we will let it can domesticate us and prevent us from taking other action.

We are domesticated when our attempts to deter the violence against us without the rule of law are discouraged by the rule of law, as two recent examples from New York illustrate. In one, lesbians collaborated with gay men and others to form a civil patrol group self-named the Pink Panthers. They are being sued for trademark infringement by the entertainment company that has the legal rights to the term *pink panther.* In a second example, lesbians collaborated with other women to attempt yet another "take back the night" march but were denied a parade permit and threatened with arrest for disorderly conduct. A "take back the night" march by "local residents" aimed at eliminating "prostitutes" from the same area was, at almost the same time, unharassed.

Thus, even when we centralize our lesbianism and demand that the legal system address the violence against us, or we attempt to address the violence apart from the legal system, we cannot be certain we are using the rules of law rather than being used by them. This does not mean that we should abandon all our strategies. In the case of the violence against us—as is the situation in most of the topics discussed in this book—legal reforms have definite positive benefits. The recognition in legal discourse that violence against lesbians counts is not insignificant, even when that counting is done in the context of legal language that manifests its own violence against us. The special approach that distinguishes acts done out of hatred for us condemns the hatred, even as it is perpetuated. The neutral approach that accords victims humanity and rejects blaming the victim is an advancement, even if it is a product of an inhumane and victimizing system.

Yet the ways in which the rule of law domesticates lesbian existence includes our own definitions of the violence against us. There is some evidence that many lesbians do not have feelings of entitlement to survival and safety regardless of what the law says. This lack of entitlement may prevent us from considering threats to our survival anything other than usual and inevitable. Within the rules of law, the very definition of crimes can limit our feelings of entitlement to safety. Lesbians need to continue to challenge the limiting of violence against us to legal crimes. From its inception, the lesbian and gay antiviolence movement, like the women against violence movement, has recognized that a violent act may not necessarily fit the elements of a criminal rule of law. The annual NGLTF Anti-Violence reports are broadly entitled "Anti-Gay/Lesbian Violence, Victimization and Defamation." They include incidents of violence that may not be criminal. Given this gap between violence and crime, proposals for the creation of new crimes such as intimidation and harassment seek to expand the rule of law's recognition and punishment of the violence against us. Another proposal is to create or increase civil liability for such acts, so that the victim could sue the perpetrator for money damages. Because such new crimes or civil causes of action often involve acts of speech, they implicate freedom of speech concerns and have caused rifts within the lesbian legal community in the same way that the pornography debates caused rifts within the lesbian/feminist community.[8]

The creation of hate crimes—as acts to be punished because they demonstrate hate—has occurred mostly in municipalities and on college campuses. Such laws generally provide for sanctions in the case of hateful activity, slurs, or epithets indicating bias. Yet because such crimes are often based upon speech or speech acts, such laws are subject to attack under constitutional free speech doctrine. The law engages in a balancing of governmental interests in preventing hate and individual rights to freedom of speech. Such a balancing act is presently being litigated before the United States Supreme Court. The case involves a challenge to a St. Paul, Minnesota ordinance criminalizing the placing of symbols, objects, or graffiti known to arouse "anger, alarm, or resentment" on the basis of "race, color, creed, religion, or gender." As in many other hate crime provisions, sexuality is omitted. The challenger to the law is a white male juvenile, charged with burning a cross on the lawn of the only African-American family in the neighborhood.[9] Many progressive organizations and advocates are divided on the preferable outcome of the case, as they are divided in many situations involving free speech.

For lesbians, the divisions in our theorizing should not necessarily be based upon First Amendment principles of free speech. The

First Amendment is a rule of law with its roots in European liberal individualism and property-based notions. Its value to lesbians must be decided by us, not assumed by us. Our thinking in this area often suffers from the internalization of the propaganda that surrounds free speech. Free speech is a "fundamental value" we like to think is enshrined within the rule of law, just like equality. Yet just as equality is not as fundamental to the rule of law as we might like to think, neither is free speech. When the speech that is supposedly free is lesbian speech, the government routinely suppresses it. Under obscenity laws, the government seizes lesbian books. In prosecutions for obscenity the word *lesbian* often appears in recitations of the titles of the books seized, as if the word alone was proof positive. In the recent National Endowment of the Arts controversy, Congress passed a law forbidding arts grants to be used to "promote, disseminate or produce" art which included depictions of "homoeroticism."[10] That lesbians and others fighting against the repression of lesbian speech often rely on the rule of law's enshrinement of free speech should not necessarily be determinative of issues relating to hate crimes involving speech.

For just as rules of law allowing the repression of speech are used against lesbians, so too are rules of law forbidding the repression of speech. It is not only that lesbians often have no legal remedy for the violent speech directed against them, including speech acts such as burning a symbol, defacing a sign, or writing antilesbian slogans, but also that when lesbians protest such acts they are condemned for their protest on the basis of a denial of free speech. Lesbians have become the quintessential "thought police" who enforce "politically correct" rules—the dominant culture domesticating us against ourselves.

The passage of rules of law that provide criminal penalties for hateful speech is problematic, and like other protections can easily be turned against us. Imagine a prosecution against a lesbian who said hateful things about a certain man's heterosexuality. Yet the presence of "speech" does not make this situation any different from the situation described earlier, in which lesbians shove a heterosexual man into a bathroom. The presence or absence of speech does not fundamentally alter the problems that lesbians face as we try to deal with the violence against us by deciding whether the rule of law can assist us or not. The rule of law that enshrines freedom of speech must be evaluated from a lesbian centered perspective and not taken as sacred in and of itself. This is not to say that we abandon strategies that might protect our lesbian speech, but only that we do not let the rule of law's speech domesticate our lesbian speech.

We must also not let the rule of law define the violence against us—define it as not-speech, as categorized, as not the rule of law itself. In order to stop the violence against us, we must define it for ourselves and then develop our lesbian strategies—both within and without the rule of law.

REFERENCES

Ruthann Robson, *Incendiary Categories: Lesbian/Violence/Law*, 2 TEXAS JOURNAL OF WOMEN AND THE LAW _____ (1992) (forthcoming).

ENDNOTES

1. The National Gay & Lesbian Task Force Policy Institute has issued annual reports entitled *Anti-Gay/Lesbian Violence, Victimization and Defamation*. Annual reports can be ordered from NGLTF at 1734 14th Street, N.W., Washington, D.C. 20009-4309, (202) 332-6483. The NGLTF also provides other information concerning proposed and enacted legislation and is a good place to start for any research into the violence against us.

  Kevin T. Berrill, with the Anti-Violence Project of NGLTF, has served as a one-person clearinghouse on the issue. His articles include, *Anti-Gay Violence and Victimization in the United States: An Overview*, 5 JOURNAL OF INTERPERSONAL VIOLENCE 274 (1990).

  Another researcher has written a book on the subject, which includes empirical data on victims and perpetrators. GARY DAVID COMSTOCK, VIOLENCE AGAINST LESBIANS AND GAY MEN (1991).

2. P.L. 101-275, 104 Stat. 140 amending 28 U.S.C. §534.

3. Quoted in Victoria Brownworth, *An Unreported Crisis*, THE ADVOCATE 50,52 (November 5, 1991).

4. N.H.REV. STAT. ANN. §651:6 (amended by Chapter 68-1990).

5. Feminist legal theory has been especially troubled by this dichotomy, which has been most pronounced in the legal treatment of women's reproductive capacity, especially pregnancy. Are women to be treated absolutely equal to men? Or do their special circumstances, like pregnancy, warrant special treatment? Absolute equality can be discriminatory, as in formulations that allow discrimination against pregnant women because all pregnant "persons" are being treated that way; the nonexistence of pregnant men is irrelevant. Special treatment can

also be discriminatory, as in formulations that allow discrimination against pregnant women for their own "protection."

6. Commonwealth v. Carr, 398 Pa. Super. 306, 580 A.2d 1362 (1990).

7. For a discussion of secondary-victimization, see Kevin Berrill, *Primary and Secondary Victimization in Anti-Gay Hate Crimes*, 5 JOURNAL OF INTERPERSONAL VIOLENCE 401 (1990).

8. I first heard the observation that the hate crimes acts may be the sex wars of the 1990s expressed by lesbian attorney Mary Dunlap.

9. R.A.V. v. St. Paul, 90-7675 (1991).

10. P.L. 101-121.

13

THE VIOLENCE AMONG US

There is not only violence against us, there is violence among us.[1] When the violence among us attracts the attention of the rule of law, it often seems as if it is our lesbianism that is being punished rather than any violent or criminal acts. Historically, this is evident in the 1721 Linck trial, in which the court noted that the "two women did not get along. Because the codefendant complained that she did not earn anything, the defendant beat her frequently."[2] However, it was not the violent expressions that prompted the rule of law to intervene but the sexual ones. The women were on trial for the crime of lesbianism.

Even in contemporary legal discourse the violence is often intertwined with our sexuality. It is our lesbianism that seems to be the real issue at trial or on appeal. For example, in two different murder convictions, the defendants raised problems with the prosecution's characterizations of them as lesbians. In a Florida case, the appellate court had no trouble rejecting the defendant's claim:

> Wiley further contends on appeal that her character was impermissibly placed in issue when the State elicited the fact that she was a "bull dagger"—a lesbian that assumes the male role during intercourse.

> This contention is without merit. The record un-
> deniably shows that the question of Wiley's sexual
> preferences came into the trial as a part of her own
> confession. According to Wiley, the victim hurled
> this invective at her during the quarrel that occurred
> between them on that fateful evening. This accusa-
> tion perhaps constitutes an explanation for the flail-
> ing received by the victim some moments later. The
> State's only crime here was to try to explain to the
> jury exactly what a bull dagger is.[3]

Although the Florida appellate court does not reveal the relationship
between the defendant and the victim—they could have just met in
the "local night spot" near where the incident occurred; they could
have been casual acquaintances arguing; they could have been best
friends; they could have been lovers—the court's interpretation of "bull
dagger" as coextensive with the "male role" illustrates the rule of law's
propensity to use lesbianism, including gender nonconformity, as
proof of violence. Likewise, in an earlier Texas case in which the victim is the defendant's putative lover—although the defendant denies
she is a lesbian—the court recites "evidence" of the lesbian relationship including that the defendant "dressed like a man, kept her hair
cut like a man, wore men's clothing, including men's shoes."[4] Not only
does such "evidence" establish the lesbianism, it implicitly establishes
the masculine partner as the violent one. Any woman who would
wear men's shoes would probably murder.

 The violence among us may be between strangers, between
friends or acquaintances, or between lovers. It is violence between
lovers that has received the most attention. In the heterosexual marriage context, it was the hard work of feminists, many of whom are
lesbians, that required the rule of law to recognize husbands' violence
against wives. Feminist agitation resulted in concrete legal reforms
such as the battered wife's defense to murder and the availability of
restraining orders for battered wives. Perhaps ironically, the identifi-
cation of violence with maleness, coupled with heterosexism and
homophobia, domesticates us as lesbians when we attempt to avail
ourselves of these concrete reforms. While this domestication may fade
in comparison to the violence we endure, or the possibility of prison,
such domestication also interferes with the benefit any of the concrete
reforms can have on our survival.

 One example is the situation of Annette Green, convicted of
murdering her lover, Ivonne Julio. The prosecutor charged Green with

first degree murder despite circumstances, including struggle in an intimate setting, that usually prompt a lesser charge. The prosecutor objected to the use of a battered woman defense despite the prosecutor's admission that Green had been "battered. She was shot at before by the victim. She had a broken nose, broken ribs." The trial judge liberally allowed the defense, however, construing it as a "battered *person* [emphasis added] defense." Thus, this 1989 Florida case marked the first time that the battered wife/battered woman defense was allowed in a case involving lesbians. Unfortunately, it took the jury only two and one-half hours to return a guilty verdict, notwithstanding the complicated issues involved. This is an unusually short time; it often takes Florida juries at least this long to even pick their foreperson. There was evidence that jury members had no inclination to extend the battered woman defense to a lesbian even before the trial began. One jury member related an incident to the judge in which two members of the jury pool spoke in the women's restroom about their desire to be selected as jurors in order to "hang that lesbian bitch." The court personnel and guards also exhibited hostility.[5]

After her conviction, Annette Green appeared on television talk shows—those quasi-legal forums—motivated by her desire to tell other lesbians to get help. Yet during those shows, she again endured attempts to domesticate her experience and channel it into acceptable legal categories:

> GERALDO: All right. Now you say there isn't role playing going on. Very often, people outside of the community would look at a relationship, and there are women who seem more butch, more masculine than others. Is that not a common thing for a more masculine partner to be with one less so?
>
> PROF. RENZETTI: No. I would say that's not a common thing, and I would say that whether or not that exists, is not necessarily related to whether or not there's battering. I'll give you an example of what I mean by that. Some of the women that I spoke with, in my study, indicated that they, as victims, were the physically smaller—no, I'm sorry—the physically larger partner. That their batterers were actually smaller than they were, and, in fact, that was one of the reasons that they were afraid to fight back, that they were afraid that they might hurt the person they loved.

> GERALDO: Annette, in your relationship, was
> Yvonne [sic] bigger or smaller than you? Who ran the
> house, generally speaking? Were you sort of the
> mother and she, roughly, kind of like the father? Is
> that the way it was?
>
> MS. GREEN: Yes. She was bigger than me. I
> worked. She stayed home most of the time. I used
> to clean, cook, do everything. I was the mother of the
> kids. I was like the wife. She was like the husband.[6]

We can change the name from battered wife to battered woman to battered person, and we can have professorial experts discuss the nature of lesbianism and violence, but jurors are like Geraldo. To successfully use a defense based on being battered, a woman must be the stereotypically good wife. Given that many heterosexual women are insufficiently wifely to sustain the defense, it is perhaps not surprising that Annette Green could not do so. Despite her failure, the forces of domestication require that Annette Green continue to force herself to fit into the legal category *wife* if she hopes to win an appeal or be granted clemency.

The legal category *wife* can be even more rigid than the liberal extension into "battered person" granted by the trial judge. Although Annette Green is on television advising other battered lesbians to get help, the help available from the legal system may be extremely limited. Annette Green herself was not entitled to any legal relief in the state where she was living because she was not within the statutory definitions of a victim of domestic abuse. She was not entitled to shelter or services from "domestic violence centers," now partially funded by the state and thus totally regulated by the state, because the relevant statute defines domestic violence as violence "by a person against the person's spouse." Further, Annette Green was not entitled to avail herself of the judicial system to obtain an injunction for protection against domestic violence. Such injunctions, often called protective orders or temporary restraining orders, are available to victims of domestic abuse in order to prevent further abuse. These civil orders have just recently become available in virtually every state, however not every state extends protection to lesbians in battering relationships. Florida, where she was living and is now imprisoned, for example, defines domestic violence as limited to "any assault, battery, or sexual battery by a person against the person's spouse or against any other person related by blood or marriage to the petitioner or respondent, who is or was residing in the same single dwelling unit."[7]

Thus, Annette Green, even if she had sought legal assistance, could not have obtained a temporary restraining order. Likewise, other states preclude lesbians as persons "unrelated by blood or marriage" from seeking protective orders, especially if there is no violence against any children in the household.[8] However, in many states—often because of recent amendments—lesbians who cohabit, or who have cohabited, may apply for protective orders in cases of domestic violence.[9] For lesbians who have never lived together, judicial protection from an abusive relationship is much more rare.[10]

Even where legal assistance is statutorily available, applications for restraining orders may be denied by courts because of the parties' lesbianism. The courts may reason that the situation is one of "mutual combat," indicating a situation where the parties are "really just fighting" rather than one in which abuse is occurring. Within the battering relationship, the concept of mutual combat may have some currency.[11] In the domestic violence movement itself, however, there is controversy about the validity of the notion of mutual combat between lesbians. The majority view is that it is a myth, and a dangerous one.[12] Another view, proposed by battered women's advocate Ginny NiCarthy, is that there are lesbians who are violent toward each other but do not ultimately succeed in controlling each other: two-way violence.[13] Under the rule of law as applied, the mutual combat concept may be more frequently used in situations in which legal officials cannot make gendered distinctions. Many judges and legal officials have been educated in domestic violence issues in ways which emphasize the dominance/submissive patriarchal arrangement based on objective criteria such as gender. When such factors are absent, judges may be more likely to feel inadequate to determine against whom the restraining order should be issued. In the face of such inadequacy, judges may either deny the restraining order or issue a mutual restraining order.

The denying of a restraining order has obvious import: the violence is deemed acceptable under the rule of law. The issuing of a mutual restraining order may have a less obvious significance. To be "restrained" from doing some act one has never done and apparently has no desire to do appears insignificant. Yet this very irrelevance conveys the message of its relevance. A mutual restraining order apportions responsibility for the violence between the parties. Despite the civil nature of the order, it serves as an adjudication that "fighting" rather than abuse is occurring.

In addition to its rhetoric, the mutual restraining order has practical legal effects. In future instances of violence, it sets a precedent, almost a "law of the case," determining that the violence between the parties is mutual. Battered women's advocates in many states have lobbied legislatures for more stringent penalties against batterers. These penalties, in order to be effective, are necessarily not limited to batterers who are convicted of crimes. If a batterer violates a civil restraining order, this itself may constitute a crime.[14] Thus, a battered lesbian who pushes her batterer in an attempt to escape through a door violates a mutual restraining order as much as the battering lesbian who barred the door. Both women may be guilty of a crime. However, even in the absence of violations of a restraining order resulting in a criminal conviction, penalties are applied to persons against whom restraining orders have been issued. In some states, a finding of "domestic violence," including findings based upon the issuance of temporary retraining orders, may disqualify one from state employment, or from employment with mental health facilities, alcohol treatment facilities, drug treatment facilities, nursing homes, child care facilities, or from working with the developmentally disabled, working with youth services, or providing foster care.[15] Thus, a mutual restraining order might impact upon one's livelihood.

Despite all the problems with concrete reforms such as restraining orders and the battered person defense, these reforms should be available to lesbians on at least the same terms as are available to heterosexual women. Of course, the sameness of the terms is problematic, given the gendered grounding of the violence against women movement which prompted the reforms. Such a gendered perspective needs to be avoided when judges or other legal officials seek to determine the aggressor in a combative relationship, unless we are prepared to accept the stereotype that lesbians who appear more masculine are always aggressors.

The violence among us calls into question the gendered grounding of the violence against women movement that has accurately and convincingly documented men's pervasive violence against women. To this extent, the rule of law can address the violence among us not only in ways that domesticate us, but also seek to domesticate any critique of male violence. The attention that lesbian battering receives from nonlesbians is therefore suspect. Such attention is often directed at proving that all of us—including women—are violent, and therefore the problem of violence is not a problem of men's violence against women. When a large part of my legal practice was advocacy on behalf of battered women, I was incessantly challenged with references to battered husbands: Had I ever represented one? Would I? And surely I would agree that men were abused by their wives? Now, it seems as if lesbians have replaced battered husbands as the category that disenables any critique of male violence.

The violence among us is a serious problem. I do not think we should tolerate threats to our survival, even when they are self-generated. Again, this requires that any reforms hard won from the rule of law should be available to lesbians. Nevertheless, as lesbians dealing with self-generated threats to our survival, we need to develop a complex discussion about our resort to the rule of law in cases of violence among us. Centering lesbians is vital, but this means centering all the lesbians involved: the ones who fit within the legal category of *perpetrator* and the ones who fit within the legal category of *victim*. At the very least, we need to remember that perpetrator and victim are categories of the rule of law.

In some cases, as when a lesbian is being prosecuted for murder, she has little choice about the extent to which she will become involved with the rule of law. In other cases, however, as when a lesbian is deciding whether or not to seek a restraining order against another lesbian, she does have choices. The choice to avail herself of any (and all) legal remedies is a choice not only supported by the rule of law, but also by the domestic violence movement. The common wisdom within the domestic violence movement is that just as one would not hesitate to seek legal recourse if assaulted by a stranger, one should not hesitate if assaulted by a lover. The choice to refuse any (and all) legal remedies is supported by lesbian separatism. As lesbians, we are aware that the rule of law and all heterosexist institutions perpetuate their own violence against us. Both the choice to use the law and the choice to avoid it are ultimately inadequate, and advocating either choice as conclusively correct is destructive to our lesbian survival.

Just as the relationship contracts discussed in chapter 10 cannot be judged as either panaceas or placebos, neither can restraining orders or similar rules of law. Again, a circumstantial approach is most likely to insure lesbian survival. An important variable in cases of violence among us is not only the individual situations of the lesbians involved, but the community context. Many lesbians have advocated that lesbian communities should "police" the violence among us with resort to various strategies, including ostracism. Putting aside questions about the ethics or effectiveness of ostracism, it presupposes a cohesive and political community. Many lesbians, however, live in relative isolation. Another important variable is the legal context. In speaking with lesbians about their experiences in seeking restraining orders, I have been amazed at differences in relatively short geographical distances, for example between San Francisco where orders are routinely granted, and the East Bay suburb of Contra Costa where lesbians have been denied restraining orders.

The rules of law regulating the violence among us also share with relationship contracts the potential to domesticate us. One type of domestication is the type evidenced by Annette Green's situation. In order to be within the rule and the spirit of her defense, she must mold herself into the legal category of *wife*. Likewise, a lesbian seeking the rule of law's remedy of a restraining order must mold herself and her (ex)lover into the categories of the statute in their particular state. In some cases, such a molding will be virtually impossible, as in the Missouri statute limiting the availability of restraining orders to violence occurring between members of the opposite sex.[16] In other cases, such a molding might be possible: a statute that limits itself to "spouses" might be broadened by a court to include lesbians in a spouselike relationship. It is true, though, that in cases which supposedly require no molding because the statute's applicability to "family or household members" is intended to include lesbians, it includes only lesbians who can analogize their relationship to recognized legal categories such as *family* or *household*.

Another type of domestication is the type discussed in the previous chapter concerning the violence against us. Our definition of violence becomes domesticated. Is a push violent? A slap? A plate thrown at a wall? What is legally sufficient to warrant a restraining order or constitute a crime becomes coextensive with our definition of violence. I am less concerned about our conclusion as to the violence of a push, slap, or thrown plate, than I am about our domestication that substitutes the rules of law for our lesbian judgments.

The last type of domestication inheres in the term *domestic violence*. Not only does lesbian domestic violence domesticate critiques of men's violence against women, but it also domesticates critiques of any systemic violence. An emphasis on domestic violence stresses individualized solutions, either within or without the rule of law. Left unexamined is the context that makes such individualized and privatized violence possible. While some lesbian commentators on the violence among us have discussed notions of power differentials, what is left unexamined is the context that produces power and power differentials—and the violence of that context.

There is violence among us. At times, whether with our consent or without it, the rule of law attempts to address this violence. We must not capitulate to the notion that violence among us requires our reflexive resort to the rule of law to solve our problems, just as we must not capitulate to the notion that the violence among us must be endured and insulated. Instead, we must develop strategies to stop the violence among us. The first strategy is to recognize how the rule of law attempts to domesticate us by using the violence among us.

REFERENCES

Ruthann Robson, *Lavender Bruises: Intra Lesbian Violence, Law and Lesbian Legal Theory*, 20 GOLDEN GATE LAW REVIEW 567 (1990).

ENDNOTES

1. NAMING THE VIOLENCE: SPEAKING OUT ABOUT LESBIAN BATTER-ING (K. Lobel, ed. Seattle, Washington: Seal Press 1986). See also Ellen Faulkner, *Lesbian Abuse: The Social and Legal Realities*, 16 QUEEN'S LAW JOURNAL 261 (1991).

2. *A Lesbian Execution in Germany, 1721: The Trial Records*, 6 J. HOMOSEXUAL-ITY 27, 32 (1980/81) (translated by Brigitte Eriksson). This trial is discussed in Chapter 2.

3. Wiley v. State, 427 So. 2d 283, 285 (Fla. 1st DCA 1983).

4. Perez v. State, 491 S.W.2d 672, 673, 675 (Tex. Crim. App. 1973).

5. Much of this information comes from Annette Green's defense attorney, William Lasley, of West Palm Beach, Florida. I appreciate his candor and cooperation.

5. Geraldo: Battered Lesbians—Battered Lovers? (television broadcast, November 21, 1989) (transcript on file). The Professor Renzetti quoted is Claire Renzetti, author of *Violence in Lesbian Relationships: A Preliminary Analysis of Causal Factors*, 3 JOURNAL OF INTERPERSONAL VIOLENCE 381 (1988).

7. The relevant Florida Statutes include Fla. Stat. 415.601-.606; Fla. Stat. §741; Fla. Stat. §741.30 (1)(a);

8. See, e.g., La. Rev. Stat. Ann. §46:2132(4) (West. 1990) (defining protectable "family or household member" as "spouses, former spouses, parents and children, stepparents, step children, foster parents, foster children, and any person living in the same residence with the defendant as a spouse, whether married or not, if a minor child or children also live in the residence who are seeking protection"); Me. Rev. Stat. Ann. tit. 15 §321(1) (1989) (defining protectable "family or household members" as "spouses or former spouses, individuals presently or formerly living as spouses, natural parents of the same child or adult household members related by consanguinity or affinity" adding that "holding one-

self out to be a spouse shall not be necessary to constitute 'living as spouses.' ");
Va. Code Ann. §16.1-228 (Supp. 1988) (extending protection to "spouse abuse"
and defining it as "committed by a person against such person's spouse, notwithstanding that such persons are separated and living apart.").

9. See, e.g., Colo. Rev. Stat. 14-4-101(2) (1987) (domestic abuse defined as violence committed or threatened by an adult or emancipated minor against another
adult or emancipated minor living "in the same domicile"); Conn. Gen. Stat.
§46b—38a(2) (West. Supp. 1990) (defining "family or household member" as including persons 16 years or older presently residing together or who have resided
together); Idaho Code §39-6303(2) (Supp. 1989) (defining "family or household
member" as including "persons who reside or who have resided together"));
Mont. Code Ann. § 40-4-121 (1988) (substituting "family or household member"
for "spouse" in 1985); N.Y. Soc. Serv. Laws §459-a (McKinney Supp. 1990) (defining "family or household members" as including "unrelated persons who are
continually or at regular intervals living in the same household" or who have
done so in the past); Pa. Cons. Stat. tit. 35 §10182 (1989) (amending the abuse
act in 1988 to include "sexual or intimate partners"); Wisc. Stat. Ann. §813.12
(West. Supp. 1989) (expanding the definition of "domestic abuse" in 1985 to include acts by a "family member or household member").

But see Mo. Rev. Stat. §455.010(5) (Supp. 1990) which did not substantially
alter Mo. Rev. Stat. §455.010(6) (protected household members as "spouses, persons related by blood or marriage, and other persons of the opposite sex jointly
residing in the same dwelling unit"); Utah Code Ann. §30-6-1 (1989) (recently
narrowed to include only "spouse" "living as spouses," "related by blood or marriage" or "having children in common" from previous 1985 amendment which
included in the "spouse abuse act" "cohabitants").

10. For an example of available protection, see Cal. Civ. Proc. Code §527.6 (West
Supp. 1990) allowing temporary retraining orders to prevent harassment.

11. As battered lesbian advocate Barbara Hart explains: "Because a battered lesbian may have used violence against her batterer and because the batterer is convinced that the victim is responsible for the batterer's abuse, it is not surprising
that many battered lesbians are confused when first contacting battered women's
advocates to break free of the violence and to establish lives outside of the control of the perpetrator. It is not surprising that they may view themselves as both
a batterer and a victim." Hart, *Lesbian Battering: An Examination* in NAMING THE
VIOLENCE at 173, 186.

12. See, e.g., *Id.* at 173.

For a critique of the concept of mutual combat between gay men, see King-
ston, *The Truth Behind Mutual Combat,* COMING UP! (now THE SAN FRAN-
CISCO BAY TIMES) Dec. 1987, at 12.

13. NiCarthy, *Lesbian Battering, Political Principles and Therapeutic Methods: Feminist Therapy Conference* (May 1987) (unpublished manuscript) (on file with author).

NiCarthy is best known for her self-help books directed toward abused
women: GETTING FREE: A HANDBOOK FOR WOMEN IN ABUSIVE RELA-
TIONSHIPS (1982) and THE ONES WHO GOT AWAY: WOMEN WHO LEFT
ABUSIVE PARTNERS (Seattle, Washington: Seal Press 1987), as well as co-
authoring with K. Merriam and S. Coffman, TALKING IT OUT: A GUIDE TO
GROUPS FOR ABUSED WOMEN (1984).

14. According to a recent survey of domestic violence statutes (which does not

include the newly enacted statutes in New Mexico and Arkansas): "Violation of a protection order constitutes civil contempt in thirty-one states, criminal contempt in twenty states and the District of Columbia, and civil and criminal contempt in eleven states. Twenty-nine states make the violation of a protection order a misdemeanor offense. Finn, *Statutory Authority in the Use and Enforcement of Civil Protections Orders Against Domestic Abuse,* 23 FAMILY LAW QUARTERLY 43, 55, (1989).

15. See, e.g., Fla. Stat. § 110.1127 (1988) (state employment); §393.0655 (caretakers for persons with developmental disabilities); §394.457 (employment in a mental health facility); §396.0425 (employment with an alcohol treatment facility); §397.0715 (employment with a drug treatment facility); §400.497 (employment with a home health agency); §402.305 (employment with a child care facility); §409.175 (providing foster care); §959.06 (employment with youth services); 1989 FLA. LAWS 535 (employment at the Florida School for the Deaf and Blind).

Additionally, a nurse may be disciplined by the state department of professional regulation for committing an "act which constitutes domestic violence as defined in §741.30." Fla. Stat. §464.018 (7)(e) (1988).

16. See Mo. Stat. §455.010 (1)(5) (1989) (defining protected household members as "spouses, former spouses, persons related by blood or marriage, persons of the *opposite sex* who are presently living together or have resided together in the past and persons who have a child in common regardless of whether they have been married or resided together at any time.").

LESBIAN CHANGE/LEGAL CHANGE

14

MEDIATION AND
ALTERNATIVE DISPUTE RESOLUTION

I f the rule of law is even half as threatening to lesbian survival as *Lesbian (Out)law* argues, then it is important to find alternatives. Alternative dispute resolution (ADR) is one often-proposed remedy, both within lesbian communities and other communities dissatisfied with the rule of law. Although ADR has many components, including arbitration and negotiation, the most popular form of ADR is mediation. Mediation is a relatively informal process in which two or more people who disagree seek to reach a mutually agreeable solution. This process is usually guided by one or more mediators. The mediator has differing roles depending upon the type of mediation, but it is not unusual for the mediator to act as a director/facilitator of the face-to-face meetings, as well as being the person responsible for documenting the agreement reached between the parties.

Mediation is especially popular in "private" disputes. The rule of law has, in some instances, enshrined mediation as a mandatory process, especially in family-type proceedings. For example, a California statute requires that divorcing couples mediate in an attempt to reach agreements about property and custody. From the court's perspective, such mandatory mediation insulates the judicial system from the messy and legally uninteresting job of applying vague rules of law to people's private lives. From the divorcing couple's perspective, mediation can save time and lawyers' fees, and provide the divorcing couple with the chance to actively participate in the solution of their own problems.

Mediation is not limited to family-type disputes, however. Throughout the country, there are both court-affiliated and community-based mediation programs that seek to resolve consumer disputes, neighborhood disputes, landlord-tenant disputes, and even environmental disputes. Mediation is also considered by many to be appropriate in cases of violence. The city of Columbus, Ohio, for example, has a much-lauded mediation program for "minor criminal disputes." There is even at least one advocate of mediation as appropriate in cases of "simple rape."[1]

Despite its increasing popularity, mediation provokes many criticisms. An important feminist critique of mediation as practiced in heterosexual divorce contexts observes how gender disparities in real life are obscured in mediation.[2] A progressive critique of mediation practiced at neighborhood dispute resolution centers observes that mediation is an alien force that inserts itself into communities, uses the discourse of communities against its own members, and ultimately discourages political organizing.[3] Both of these critiques are basically concerned with mediation's tendency to privatize and individualize disputes and are relevant for any lesbian-centered perspective on mediation.

The dangers of mediation's privatization/individualization tendency are readily apparent in situations of mediation between lesbians and nonlesbians. For example, if a lesbian were to mediate claims of sexual orientation discrimination by her employer, the lesbian might very well find herself in a mediation session in which the employer's biases are reduced to personal quirks unconnected to oppressive cultural forces. Almost all mediation proponents agree that notions of right or wrong and guilt or innocence are not important to the mediation process. Thus, a lesbian involved in mediation is not entitled to any political or moral claim that homophobia is wrong. The lesbian's status as a lesbian and the employer's status as a homophobe are both made virtually irrelevant. The employer and the lesbian would be urged to address particular aspects of their dispute that might be cured. That the employer's specific objections to this lesbian—for example, that she is aggressive or does not dress "properly"—might be connected to stereotypes can be safely ignored. The lesbian would be compelled to take into account the employer's feelings about her attitude and dress so that there can be a mutually acceptable agreement on these issues. If the lesbian claimed that the employer's objections were homophobic, she would commit the mediation sin of unproductive blaming. Such a scenerio serves the interest of the state because it forestalls political action. The potential mediation of cases not only of discrimination but also of violence—including "simple rape"—against lesbians allows the state to effectively remove such situations from public discourse.

The effects of privatization and individualization are also problematic when the dispute is between lesbians. Mediation effectively precludes any political claims based upon racism, classism, anti-Semitism, ageism, or ableism. Further, because mediation is negotiation designed to produce as its end-product an agreement, it suffers from the same problems as the relationship contracts discussed in chapter 10. There is an assumption of formal equality, that all disputants have equal feelings of entitlement, and that all are able to effectively negotiate. This formal equality may have a very low denominator if one credits mediators' statements that women do not know how to negotiate, are too concerned with being politically correct, and even that they are too vindictive to negotiate correctly. The presence of the mediator might assist lesbians in learning to play the quasi-legal game called negotiation, but it does not insure that any real power disparities will be addressed. Mediators are wary of injecting their own notions of fairness into the agreement given mediation's purpose of producing an agreement based on the parties' notions of fairness.

The end-product contract also shares the domesticating quality of the relationship contract. In place of lesbian-generated solutions, there is a prescribed methodology of resolving disputes. Although an alternative to legal dispute resolution, mediation is often derivative of legal process. The law looms large through its circumvention. In heterosexual divorce cases, the mediation process is often designed to produce an agreement substantially similar to the one the parties' lawyers would have negotiated or the judgment the court would have imposed. If this analogy is applied to lesbian couples, the mediation process might be akin to a heterosexual divorce: mediation as designed to produce an agreement substantially similar to the one the parties' lawyers would have negotiated or the judgment the court would have imposed if the couple were heterosexual rather than lesbian. When lesbian couples have children, the analogy to heterosexual couples ends. Absent adoption, one lesbian will have greater status vis-à-vis the child than the other, and the mediation occurs against this backdrop. I have heard of the biological lesbian mother agreeing to mediation while saying she will not agree to virtually anything that her ex-lover desires because as biological mother she has all the rights. In many cases, mediation becomes a substitute for litigation, but not a meaningful—or lesbian—alternative.

Lesbian alternatives are just beginning to be articulated, although it is true that as outlaws, we have been resolving our own disputes for many years. I would like to propose an ideal system of dispute resolution, especially for the disputes that arise between lesbians, but I cannot. I am only beginning to appreciate my own domestication and realize how much my thinking is dominated by legal categories, including "alternative" legal categories. I think that as we become aware of how our lesbian imaginations have been limited by our domestication, we will begin to formulate possibilities that I cannot presently envision.

For now, however, this is not to say that lesbians should never mediate. Just as relationship contracts can be an empowering option for lesbians, so can mediation. There may even be something inherently empowering about solving a dispute without resort to the formal rule of law. Yet I am also suspicious that this empowerment is most profoundly experienced by the mediator rather than by the disagreeing lesbians.

The role of the mediator is problematic from a lesbian-centered perspective. Both within and outside of lesbian communities, the training of mediators is stressed. One aspect of this training is to teach the mediator to recognize her own biases. The training assumes that no one is bias-free, and therefore the best a mediator can do is acknowledge her own biases. The character of this acknowledgment varies. Some mediation theories relegate this acknowledgment to part of the mediator's internal processes. For the mediator to say to the clients, for example, that she believes all lesbian couples who separate should remain friends, would be impermissibly injecting her own bias into the mediation. Other mediation theories stress that this acknowledgment should be part of the mediation process. The mediator thus shares her own bias that the separating couple remain friends. In either case, however, the bias surfaces in exactly the type of situation in which biases are most likely to flourish: the private setting. The larger question is why any particular bias should or should not be encouraged. Perhaps lesbians would like to instill such a friendship value into mediation between lesbians. Or perhaps not. By naming values as peculiar biases of the mediator, they are unconnected to any active or political analysis or imagining of lesbianism. The process is particularly individualized and privatized.

Management of bias is only one aspect of mediation training. Training is what makes mediators experts. Many of the conversations

I have had with both lesbian and nonlesbian mediators often devolve into a recitation of their qualifications. There are organizations, academic articles, manuals, a movement for standardized trainings, and certifications. There is increasing professionalization.

According to lesbian theorist Barbara MacDonald, lesbians can build careers by exploiting other lesbians. We turn each other into clients as we apply the "skills" certified by the dominant culture. We may have a sincere desire to help each other, but our process is one that Barbara MacDonald judges depoliticizing and disempowering.[4] It is one aspect of what I have called domestication.

Mediators as professional problem solvers bear a striking resemblance to therapists. While mediation developed as an alternative to the rule of law, it has been heavily influenced by therapeutic models. In *Lesbian Psychologies*, a lesbian attorney and therapist talk about their joint practice of mediating disputes among lesbians. The therapist considers the mediation process similar to therapy, while the attorney considers it circumventing the patriarchal nature of litigation yet still producing a legally enforceable contract.[5] Their four-hundred-dollar fees (in 1984) are less expensive when compared to litigation, and even when compared to therapy, but what about when compared to friendship? Just as therapists have been subject to accusations of being "paid friends," mediators can also be similarly categorized. Therapists and mediators are credentialed by institutions and organizations that are hostile—or at the very least extraneous—to lesbians. When we put lesbians at the center, such professionalism operates as an agent of domestication.

Of course, the same can be said of the professionals who are lesbian legal workers. The next chapter considers lesbians who work with the law.

ENDNOTES

1. See *Using Mediation in Cases of Simple Rape*, 47 WASHINGTON & LEE LAW REV. 1183 (1990).

2. See Trina Grillo, *The Mediation Alternative: Process Dangers for Women*, 100 YALE LAW JOURNAL 1545 (1991).

3. Richard Delgado has been the most vociferous proponent of this critique. His works include *ADR and the Dispossessed*, 13 LAW AND SOCIAL INQUIRY 145 (1988).

4. Barbara MacDonald's ideas on this topic were presented in a speech at the National Lesbian Conference in April 1991, and the speech is published as *Professionalism Is Not Benign*, SOJOURNER: THE WOMEN'S FORUM at 10P (June 1991).

5. Bonnie Englehardt and Katherine Triantafillou, *Mediation for Lesbians* in LESBIAN PSYCHOLOGIES (ed. Boston Lesbian Psychologies Collective 1987).

15

LESBIAN LEGAL WORKERS

W e are judges, court reporters, hearing officers, community activists, lawyers, paralegals, legal secretaries, teachers, librarians, and students. We are former legal workers who now do general academic support, run retail shops, pursue acting careers, and publish books. We are going to law school, attending a paralegal program, learning court reporting. We have cultural affinities, religious preferences, racial identities, and class backgrounds. We are idealistic, cynical, disillusioned, stubborn, tired, and comfortable. We build legal careers around our lesbianism, and we erect legal careers around our lesbian closets.

Historically, we are a recent phenomenon. Although women have been welcomed within the ranks of supporting workers doing most of the work for fractions of the pay, women were routinely excluded from positions as paralegals, court reporters, and lawyers. There were a few women attorneys allowed to practice law in various states, but the United States Supreme Court in 1872 had no trouble affirming a state's right to exclude women from the practice of law: "The paramount destiny and mission of women are to fulfil the noble and benign offices of wife and mother. This is the law of the Creator."[1] Until the late 1960s, most state bars, state law schools, and private law schools had a policy of excluding women, an exclusion which resulted in 97-98 percent of all attorneys being male. Of the few women attorneys, about twenty-five were women of color.[2] We have no statistics about the number of lesbians who were attorneys. Obviously, the minimal number of women attorneys could result in only a minimal number of lesbian attorneys. Lesbian presence within this group was further limited by a legal climate which barely recognized lesbian possibility. If women attorneys were an "invisible bar,"[3] as one historian claims, then lesbian attorneys were invisible even within that invisible bar.

Yet lesbian attorneys existed. For example, Anyda Marchant attended National Law School, a privately owned law school that admitted women, on a scholarship funded by the Women's Bar Association of the District of Columbia. When she graduated in 1936, she practiced with a small firm and then worked at the Law Library of Congress during World War II. When the male attorney whose position she had filled returned from soldiering, she lost her job. Over the next several decades, she practiced law in an international context, with positions in Brazil, in a large law firm, in a department of the United States government, and eighteen years in the legal department of an international agency. Yet Anyda Marchant is not only a model of the survival of lesbian lawyers, but a model of the survival of lesbian spirit. During the time she was lawyering, she was also writing fiction. When she retired from the law in 1972, she founded the lesbian publishing house, Naiad Press.[4] Naiad continues to publish the elegant lesbian novels of Sarah Aldridge, the pen name of Anyda Marchant.

In what ways Anyda Marchant is typical or atypical of the lesbian lawyers who survived in a profession of 2-3 percent women is difficult to determine. Yet it is just as difficult to construct a composite of the contemporary lesbian legal worker. We are prone to think about the most visible lesbian legal workers, those who have devoted their considerable energies to advocating on behalf of lesbian rights. There is Roberta Achtenburg, past director of the Lesbian Rights Project and presently a San Francisco elected official; Mary Dunlap, a private attorney in San Francisco; Paula Ettlebrick, legal director of the Lambda Legal Defense and Education Fund; Elizabeth Hendrickson, the current director of the Lesbian Rights Project, recently renamed the National Center for Lesbian Rights; Sandra Lowe, former attorney with Lambda Legal Defense Fund and recently named the director of the New York Governor's newly created Office of Gay and Lesbian Concerns; Abby Rubenfeld, former director of Lambda Legal Defense Fund and now an attorney in private practice in Nashville;

and M.P. Shildmeyer, an attorney in private practice in Atlanta. There is Donna Hitchins, the first openly lesbian judge. There are law professors Pat Cain and Jean Love, both recently relocated to the University of Iowa; Barbara Cox at California Western; Nancy Polikoff at American University; and Rhonda Rivera, a pioneering lesbian law professor at Ohio State. There are the attorneys, paralegals, and support workers working for or affiliated with legal advocacy organizations such as the previously mentioned National Center for Lesbian Rights and Lambda Legal Defense and Education Fund, as well as the ACLU Gay and Lesbian Rights Project and the National Gay and Lesbian Task Force. There are many, many more lesbian legal workers who do advocacy work on behalf of other lesbians, both in "test" cases and in individual cases within their own communities. Usually, advocacy for lesbians is combined with advocacy for gay men, and even the National Center for Lesbian Rights has litigated on behalf of gay men.

Yet there are also many lesbian legal workers who are not primarily involved in advocacy for lesbians. We are public defenders and poverty law attorneys. I have always suspected that a great number of us are involved in legal work directed at the disenfranchised. An informal survey I sent out to identified lesbian legal workers confirms this suspicion, but such a confirmation is itself suspect. The names of the survey recipients were obtained from lists of women members of lesbian/gay legal associations or distributed at lesbian/gay legal events, as well as from friends of friends. I never intended the survey to be a sociologically sophisticated statistical sample. Thus, it is impossible to make assumptions about lesbian legal workers' propensity to practice public interest law based on such a self-selected group of fifty-two survey respondents. Further, even within this limited sampling, there was a sprinkling of lesbians practicing other types of law: a prosecutor, a staff attorney for a federal court, a personal injury attorney, a lesbian legal worker employed by the county, and a few lesbians involved in business litigation.

Within this self-selected sampling of survey respondents, there was an amazing array of opinions. Of those who had been lesbians before their legal work, most thought that working within the law made them more lesbian-identified. About half of these responses contained statements indicating that lesbianism increased their desires and ability to "fight for justice," "obtain true equality," or "be sensitive to clients." Other responses, however, indicated that working within the law made them less lesbian-identified, and a few responses related instances of going "back into the closet." Several lesbian legal workers felt that their lesbianism did not affect their legal work, and that their legal work did not affect their lesbianism. Many lesbians doing legal advocacy on behalf of lesbians and gay men expressed intense satisfaction, while many others felt that lesbians were tokenized by gay male concerns. Many lesbians expressed dedication to advocacy on behalf of all people of color, in poverty, and other disenfranchised groups, but most of the lesbian legal workers expressing this dedication also expressed the perception that such work was not taken seriously enough within lesbian legal circles.

Almost all of the responses emphasized pro-active legal work, including litigation, agreements, estate planning, and mediation. This work centered on what the respondents most often described as "family law," which included custody, adoption, relationship contracts, domestic violence, and domestic partnerships. Only one respondent mentioned legal scholarship, although several of the respondents were in academia. When asked about what topics not covered in the survey they would like to have treated in a book on lesbian legal issues, more than half of the respondents did not reply. Of those who did reply, I am grateful for their advice—which I took in every instance.

The surveys assisted me tremendously, providing insights and enthusiasm. Based on these surveys, I asked several lesbian legal workers to complete longer reflections and interviewed several other lesbian legal workers. This work was also inspirational. Our choices as lesbian legal workers continue to fascinate me.

Yet I also continue to wonder about the choices of those lesbian legal workers who would never respond to such a survey. Their names are not on any lists of legal workers interested in lesbian or lesbian/gay legal issues. Their names are not passed on by friends of friends. Sometimes, however, I know them. Or knew them.

She worked with a medium-sized firm. As a rather new associate attorney, her major client was a public housing authority. Her job was to evict my clients, tenants who lived below the poverty line and qualified for public housing as well as for free legal services. She and I negotiated case after case, year after year. We threatened each other with complicated legal memoranda and the possibility of convoluted trials. I perceived her as an enemy. I knew she was a lesbian even before I saw her in a local lesbian bar. I did not talk to her in the bar because I judged her legal work as oppositional to her lesbianism. After that, she suggested we might "play tennis" sometime. I rudely responded that she could call me after she quit representing slumlords. She never called me, except about more evictions.

Our respective positions within the rule of law were antagonistic. We never really recognized each other as dykes across the divide. If we had centered our lesbianism instead of landlord/tenant law, we would have had a different relationship. Yet such a centering seemed impossible to me at the time. And it still seems difficult, given my notions of lesbianism as including a commitment to eradicating the classism and racism evidenced in the eviction actions. Such expansive notions of lesbianism are being debated by lesbian theorists and activists every day. Such debates can make the possibility of combining theory and activism difficult, as discussed in chapter 1.

Despite our differences, what she and I shared as lesbians was our domestication by the rule of law. I am not suggesting that she and I shared some common lesbian essence, but that we had both subjected ourselves to the domesticating forces of the legal profession. For those of us who have attended law school, the domestication is presented in positive terms as our professionalization. It does not matter whether we are drawn to the law in order to do social good or in order to support ourselves, we were selected by a process that prides itself on its elitism. Standards like grade point averages and scores on the standardized tests (LSAT) screen out applicants who do not demonstrate facility in the analytic methodologies prized within the rule of law. Selection itself does not insure education: scholarships are more rare than one would expect, financial aid depends on arbitrary federal educational policies and economic factors, and even public law schools are exorbitantly expensive.

Once admitted, traditional law schools attempt to terrorize students into brilliant conformity—conformity being preferred over brilliance. Imagination, independence, and individuality are eradicated. Dominant definitions prevail as rationality and neutrality. These are enforced through keen competition for the top grades on a mandatory and artificial curve and threats of failure, academic dismissal, or unemployment. Learning to "think like a lawyer," the enunciated goal of a legal education, means learning to think like the stereotype of a lawyer as a white, straight, upper-class male, preferably Protestant and able-bodied enough to play golf. Political perspectives are discouraged, and emotions exist to be manipulated. Thinking like a lawyer includes the ability to argue any side of any issue.

In my first "trial," a simulated case during a criminal law clinical course, the professor assigned me to prosecute a woman who had allegedly shot her husband while he was assaulting her for the hundredth time. I did a commendable job, even making a few sophisticated evidentiary objections. The major criticism, however, was that I did not display sufficient zealousness. The professor told me that he knew I would hate prosecuting the woman, but that he thought I would learn a lot. He was especially interested in teaching me that I could do something well even if it was a cause in which I did not believe. He assured me that with practice, I could learn to demonstrate more zealousness.

I agreed then and still agree that I learned a lot, including the intended lesson. Much of my agreement is attributable to the ways in which I have been domesticated by lawyering skills training. As a teacher, I am often tempted to repeat this lesson on my lesbian law students. After all, I want them to be able to "think like lawyers." I become an agent of their domestication.

Resisting my own participation in domestication has meant that I never represented a client whose cause I found inconsistent with what I named lesbianism. I certainly represented clients I did not like and made arguments based on laws I found distasteful, but the lesson that I could do an adequate job representing a position I found abhorrent terrified me. Resisting my complicity in domesticating others has meant that I choose to teach at an alternative law school. A straight white male student in a constitutional theory course, beleaguered to be in a minority for the first time in his life, complained that the exam questions I gave were not sufficiently neutral. The students were always assigned to represent some "black lesbian unwed mother" charging constitutional violations, rather than assigned to defend the state that was being charged with discriminating. For this student, at least, I am repeating the experience I had of representing a cause I found politically abhorrent. Perhaps I am fooling myself not to label this process domestication, but despite the power differentials between student and professor, I perceive his complaint as an attempt to domesticate me and my hypothetical "black lesbian unwed mother."

I offer my personal experiences not as blueprint or confession, but as a specific examination of the ways in which domestication is ongoing and insidious. It is often easy to judge others as domesticated: blue suits and pumps, corporate jobs and VCRs, carpeted offices with photographs of parents but not lovers, clients complete with cultured accents and hearty heterosexism. However, even those of us with intentions to center lesbianism rather than the rule of law have difficulties sustaining our course.

I am domesticated by my stake in the rules of law. I have invested a great deal of time, money, and energy into learning legal analysis and legal methodologies, as well as specific rules of law. I think like a lawyer. My thinking not only pays the rent and allows me to buy food and books, but it affords me status within the dominant culture as well as within lesbian communities. I have become accustomed to this status. When a friend tells me about a problem she is having, I analyze it for its legal consequences. When it does not have any legal consequences, I analyze it as if it did. I have internalized my position as a "counselor of law," and relate to her in that way. It does not matter that I do not charge her money; I will accept her deference as sufficient payment.

It is easy for us to submit to our own domestication when this domestication affords us privilege. Lesbian legal workers, especially those professionalized as attorneys, judges, and law professors, have a stake in maintaining the rule of law because it maintains our own status as professionals. The survey questionnaire had a list of topics asking for responses, one of which was *lesbian separatism*. One lesbian attorney condemned it with the single word *unprofessional*. Such a reductive analysis of any facet of lesbianism marks our domestication.

For lesbian legal workers who are not accorded the status of professionals, the elitism of lesbian professionals can be painful. Again, the rule of law divides us against ourselves. Here are the comments of Linda Rothfield, a lesbian legal secretary, about her relationship with a lesbian attorney working in the same small law firm:

> When the new lesbian attorney began in the fall, I approached her in a mild manner to have lunch together. I felt that it might be nice for both of us to get to know each other (as I believed us to be the only two lesbians in my firm) and for her to know someone she didn't need to hide from. However, since that first lunch, any other lunch has been out of the question as she consistently ignores me or tries to avoid me whenever she can. This I believe is for two reasons. As an out lesbian, I potentially pose a threat to her "in the closet" status as guilt by association becomes a major factor. Also, as I am "only" a legal secretary, it simply may be that like most attorneys, she feels that professionally I am beneath her and wants nothing to do with me. I have been told by an associate attorney in the firm that this lawyer was advised not to associate with the secretarial staff. It is a ridiculous situation from my standpoint, and one which I see no hope of rectifying.

The distances between us evident in a traditional law firm are not necessarily diminished when we are outside of that setting. Linda

Rothfield relates her initial hope when she read an ad about the forming of a lesbian and gay law association, welcoming "all attorneys, law
students and other legal workers." At the conference, however, she was
only one of three paralegals or legal secretaries present, and "we were
jeered at and disregarded when we expressed our opinions or
demanded that we be represented equally in the bylaws. I felt totally
worthless when I left this event."

Our professionalism not only divides us against each other,
it divides us from our own imaginations. A survey question asked lesbian legal workers how they would combine their lesbianism and their
legal careers in "an ideal world," with a parenthetical instruction to "be
as wild and creative as you want." We were not very wild and creative. Most of the responses focused on improving one's individual
circumstances—more money or the ability to be more "out"—although
this was often blended with a desire to have a more consistently lesbian or lesbian/gay client base. It was not until I read a response from
a lesbian paralegal concerning her ideal world as not needing any legal careers that I perceived our inability to even imagine an ideal world
without the law; that I perceived the domestication inherent in the
question as I had posed it.

Our domestication by the rule of law has centralized the rule
of law in our own thinking. We cannot imagine lesbianism, or life,
without it. We do not challenge a question that assumes the ideal
world and the rule of law are inextricably bound. We think like
lawyers.

Our lawyerly thinking can produce concrete reforms that assist our survival under the rule of law. We argue our lesbianism into
more advantageous categories because we do not want lesbians to be
imprisoned, executed, separated from lovers or children, investigated,
or discriminated against. We compress lesbianism into categories that
the law recognizes are the categories of those who deserve the law's
protection, of those who deserve to survive.

Despite this domestication, we lesbians are resisters of the
rule of law. So many of the survey responses and longer reflections
were testaments of survival, not only individual but collective lesbian
survival. We quit the law, we went back to it. We changed jobs. We
helped other lesbians and we acknowledged our help from other lesbians. We described ourselves: a Puerto Rican lesbian from the Bronx;
a lesbian-daughter of a lawyer-father; a "late blooming" lesbian who
started law school at thirty-five and came out at forty-one; a "lesbian
outlaw" before being a "lesbian lawyer"; a lesbian who felt excluded
in law school because of her class background rather than her lesbi-

anism; a lesbian separatist novelist attorney; a white lesbian public defender dedicated to exposing the racism of the criminal justice system; a lesbian legal secretary, raised to be a lawyer but pursuing an acting career. We decried the mainstreaming of our lesbianism and the tokenization of our concerns in progressive legal circles. We examined our own complicities and acknowledged our own elitisms. We expressed a desire for a better life for all lesbians, even the ones we did not like. We expressed desire.

A desire that is not domesticated by legal categories. A desire that is not reducible to homosexuality or sexual orientation. A desire that is not contained by our exemplary behavior as good mothers, good soldiers, or professionals. A desire that we are not victims to be counted but not encouraged, not the perpetrators of unmentionable acts, not the subjects of someone else's free speech. A desire that our relationships are not quasi-marriages, quasi-families, or quasi-anythings. A desire that is neither equality nor inequality, neither immutable nor changeable, neither public nor private. A desire that provokes censure, criminal sanctions, executions, and possible protections from the rule of law. A desire that is not singular; desires that are not defined by the places we put our fingers, our tongues, our possessions. Desires that mark us as our own (out)laws.

ENDNOTES

1. Bradwell v. Illinois, 83 U.S. (16 Wall.) 1872.

2. DEBORAH RHODE, JUSTICE AND GENDER 23 (1990).

3. KAREN BERGER MORELLO, THE INVISIBLE BAR: THE WOMAN LAWYER IN AMERICA: 1638 TO THE PRESENT (1986). Lesbian invisibility is perpetuated in this history, which contains no index entry for lesbianism.

4. Naiad Press, the oldest and largest lesbian publishing company, was incorporated several years later by Anyda Marchant, along with Muriel Inez Crawford, her life-companion since 1948, and Barbara Grier as shareholders. Donna McBride joined them soon after.

Other titles from Firebrand Books include:

Artemis In Echo Park, Poetry by Eloise Klein Healy/$8.95
Beneath My Heart, Poetry by Janice Gould/$8.95
The Big Mama Stories by Shay Youngblood/$8.95
A Burst Of Light, Essays by Audre Lorde/$7.95
Cecile, Stories by Ruthann Robson/$8.95
Crime Against Nature, Poetry by Minnie Bruce Pratt/$8.95
Diamonds Are A Dyke's Best Friend by Yvonne Zipter/$9.95
Dykes To Watch Out For, Cartoons by Alison Bechdel/$6.95
Dykes To Watch Out For: The Sequel, Cartoons by Alison Bechdel
    /$8.95
Exile In The Promised Land, A Memoir by Marcia Freedman/$8.95
Eye Of A Hurricane, Stories by Ruthann Robson/$8.95
The Fires Of Bride, A Novel by Ellen Galford/$8.95
Food & Spirits, Stories by Beth Brant (*Degonwadonti*)/$8.95
Free Ride, A Novel by Marilyn Gayle/$9.95
A Gathering Of Spirit, A Collection by North American Indian
    Women edited by Beth Brant (*Degonwadonti*)/$10.95
Getting Home Alive by Aurora Levins Morales and Rosario
    Morales/$8.95
The Gilda Stories, A Novel by Jewelle Gomez/$9.95
Good Enough To Eat, A Novel by Lesléa Newman/$8.95
Humid Pitch, Narrative Poetry by Cheryl Clarke/$8.95
Jewish Women's Call For Peace edited by Rita Falbel, Irena Klepfisz,
    and Donna Nevel/$4.95
Jonestown & Other Madness, Poetry by Pat Parker/$7.95
Just Say Yes, A Novel by Judith McDaniel/$8.95
The Land Of Look Behind, Prose and Poetry by Michelle Cliff/$8.95
Legal Tender, A Mystery by Marion Foster/$9.95
A Letter To Harvey Milk, Short Stories by Lesléa Newman/$8.95
Letting In The Night, A Novel by Joan Lindau/$8.95
Living As A Lesbian, Poetry by Cheryl Clarke/$7.95
Making It, A Woman's Guide to Sex in the Age of AIDS by Cindy
    Patton and Janis Kelly/$4.95
Metamorphosis, Reflections On Recovery by Judith McDaniel/$7.95
Mohawk Trail by Beth Brant (*Degonwadonti*)/$7.95
Moll Cutpurse, A Novel by Ellen Galford/$7.95
The Monarchs Are Flying, A Novel by Marion Foster/$8.95
More Dykes To Watch Out For, Cartoons by Alison Bechdel/$7.95
Movement In Black, Poetry by Pat Parker/$8.95

My Mama's Dead Squirrel, Lesbian Essays on Southern Culture by Mab Segrest/$9.95

New, Improved! Dykes To Watch Out For, Cartoons by Alison Bechdel /$7.95

The Other Sappho, A Novel by Ellen Frye/$8.95

Out In The World, International Lesbian Organizing by Shelley Anderson/$4.95

Politics Of The Heart, A Lesbian Parenting Anthology edited by Sandra Pollack and Jeanne Vaughn/$11.95

Presenting. . . Sister NoBlues by Hattie Gossett/$8.95

Rebellion, Essays 1980-1991 by Minnie Bruce Pratt/$10.95

A Restricted Country by Joan Nestle/$8.95

Sacred Space by Geraldine Hatch Hanon/$9.95

Sanctuary, A Journey by Judith McDaniel/$7.95

Sans Souci, And Other Stories by Dionne Brand/$8.95

Scuttlebutt, A Novel by Jana Williams/$8.95

Shoulders, A Novel by Georgia Cotrell/$8.95

Simple Songs, Stories by Vickie Sears/$8.95

Speaking Dreams, Science Fiction by Severna Park/$9.95

The Sun Is Not Merciful, Short Stories by Anna Lee Walters/$7.95

Tender Warriors, A Novel by Rachel Guido deVries/$8.95

This Is About Incest by Margaret Randall/$8.95

The Threshing Floor, Short Stories by Barbara Burford/$7.95

Trash, Stories by Dorothy Allison/$8.95

The Women Who Hate Me, Poetry by Dorothy Allison/$8.95

Words To The Wise, A Writer's Guide to Feminist and Lesbian Periodicals & Publishers by Andrea Fleck Clardy/$4.95

The Worry Girl, Stories From A Childhood by Andrea Freud Loewenstein/$8.95

Yours In Struggle, Three Feminist Perspectives on Anti-Semitism and Racism by Elly Bulkin, Minnie Bruce Pratt, and Barbara Smith/$8.95

You can buy Firebrand titles at your bookstore, or order them directly from the publisher (141 The Commons, Ithaca, New York 14850, 607-272-0000).

Please include $2.00 shipping for the first book and $.50 for each additional book.

A free catalog is available on request.